NEW GERMAN CINEMA

IMAGES OF A GENERATION

JULIA KNIGHT

WALLFLOWER

LONDON and NEW YORK

A Wallflower Paperback

First published in Great Britain in 2004 by Wallflower Press
4th Floor, 26 Shacklewell Lane, London E8 2EZ
www.wallflowerpress.co.uk

A catalogue record for this book is available from the British Library

ISBN 1 903364 28 0

Book Design by Rob Bowden Design

Printed in Great Britain by Antony Rowe Ltd, Chippenham, Wiltshire

SHORT CUTS

INTRODUCTIONS TO FILM STUDIES

CONTENTS

LIST OF ILLUSTRATIONS

ACKNOWLEDGEMENTS

I would like to thank my colleagues in the Department of Media Arts at the University of Luton for their support and assistance while writing this book, Yoram Allon at Wallflower Press for his patience, and the students I have taught over the years.

Deep, heartfelt thanks also go to my family, especially Lance Davenport for all his support and forbearance, and to Sam and Jake.

This book is dedicated to Lance.

INTRODUCTION

In 1966, a cheaply produced, black and white feature film by a West German lawyer made cinema history. The film, *Yesterday Girl (Abschied von gestern*, 1965–66) by Alexander Kluge, won the Special Jury Prize at the Venice Film Festival and was nominated for its Gold Lion award. This made it the first German film to win such critical recognition at the prestigeous festival since the founding of the Federal Republic nearly twenty years earlier. The ideologically tainted films of the Nazi era, together with an unremarkable output during the 1950s, had left German cinema little to be proud of since the expressionist films of the 1920s. Hence Kluge's achievement was particularly noteworthy – and quickly followed by others. During the next two years Kluge went on to win Venice's Gold Lion award with his second feature, *Artistes at the Top of the Big Top: Disorientated (Die Artisten in der Zirkuskuppel: Ratlos*, 1967), and other new young West German directors also garnered an unprecedented number of festival prizes, awards and commendations.

This trend continued into and throughout the 1970s, resulting in a growing interest among film critics and establishing a handful of directors – in particular Rainer Werner Fassbinder, Wim Wenders and Werner Herzog – as 'stars' on the international film festival and art cinema circuits. The reputations of some directors were also fuelled by colourful stories of eccentric or extreme behaviour. Herzog, for instance, was reported to have walked all the way from Munich to Paris in 1974 to see elderly film critic

Lotte Eisner when he heard she was dangerously ill, while Fassbinder was dubbed a *Wunderkind* due to his obsessive approach to work and prolific output.

This batch of critically acclaimed films spanned some 15–20 years, roughly from the mid-1960s to the early 1980s, and have generally become known as the New German Cinema. Although grouped together under this umbrella term, the films resist clear generic delineation and are in fact stylistically and thematically very diverse. Interestingly, critics have accounted for this diversity by identifying – broadly speaking – three common elements that nevertheless unite the films. Firstly, their directors were all born around the time of the Second World War, grew up in a divided Germany, and can hence be characterised as a generation. Thomas Elsaesser has suggested therefore that the cinema's diversity was 'an attempt to gather, record and report the images, sounds and stories ... which make up the memory of a generation, a nation and a culture' (1989: 322). Secondly, most studies of the New German Cinema draw attention to the fact that due to the funding criteria and opportunities, the cinema was based on an artisanal mode of production which allowed a high degree of experimentation and close collaborations. And lastly, Timothy Corrigan (1994: 169) has argued, as has Elsaesser (1989: 52), that the search for audiences and movie markets was a shared characteristic which helped determine the heterogeneity of the films that constituted this new cinema.

Diverse though the films may be, these features helped mark them out as a distinctive and specifically national cinema. And when Volker Schlöndorff's *The Tin Drum* (*Die Blechtrommel*, 1979) won the highly coveted Academy Award for Best Foreign Language Film in 1980, it seemed to cement the New German Cinema's position on the international cinema scene. Indeed, that same year one British critic described it as 'one of the most remarkable, enduring and promising developments in the cinema of the 1970s' (Sandford 1981: 6).[1] Yet within the space of a few years, critics were starting to proclaim the death of the New German Cinema. Films made by its directors in the mid-1980s were arousing far less interest than their previous work and, as Elsaesser puts it, 'the feeling became inescapable that the central impulse of a distinctly national cinema had been lost' (1989: 309).

This dramatic rise and fall in the fortunes of West German film prompts three major questions, and it is these questions which shape this introductory study. Firstly, how did the New German Cinema come into existence? Awareness in Britain and the US of this new phase in the history of German cinema started to develop during the mid-1970s. In February 1976, for instance, the US magazine *Newsweek* ran an article entitled 'The German Film Renaissance', while a few months later the BBC featured the new cinema in an *Omnibus* report entitled 'Vigorous Signs of Life'. These early accounts tended to suggest that this 'renaissance' had been brought about solely through the endeavours of a small number of talented and dedicated young directors. Typical of the descriptions of German cinema's rebirth was that offered by *Time* magazine in 1978:

> With little encouragement, less money and no older hands to guide them, a few extraordinary young directors have given birth to a phoenix – the brilliant German cinema of Fritz Lang and Ernst Lubitsch that Hitler had consigned to the ashes forty-five years ago. (Clarke 1978: 51)

In keeping with this approach, many observers focused on the personalities of the new directors, discussing them as creative geniuses, 'artists with something to say' (Eidsvik 1979: 174). And the films were initially discussed almost exclusively in terms of their directors' personal visions, with the cinema heralded as a 'cinéma des auteurs'. While the first major studies to be published – such as those by John Sandford (1981) and in academic journals such as *Literature/Film Quarterly* (1979), *Wide Angle* (1980), *Quarterly Review of Film Studies* (1980) and *New German Critique* (1981–82) – started to offer some background information, they nevertheless tended to concentrate on profiling a handful of the better-known film-makers, usually Fassbinder, Wenders, Herzog, Kluge, Schlöndorff and Hans-Jürgen Syberberg.

As subsequent studies have shown, however, this auteurist approach gives only a very partial understanding of how and why a particular cinema movement or body of films has come into existence. The work of, for instance, Timothy Corrigan (1983, 1994), Eric Rentschler (1984, 1986),

Thomas Elsaesser (1989), Anton Kaes (1989), Richard W. McCormick (1991), Julia Knight (1992), Sandra Frieden *et al.* (1993), and Ingeborg Majer O'Sickey and Ingeborg von Zadow (1998) demonstrates that a whole range of historical, cultural, social, political, economic, institutional and gender-related factors also helped shape the New German Cinema. Moreover, in contrast to the view expressed by the *Time* writer quoted above, a number of these studies also contextualise some of the New German Cinema films within wider historical, cultural and political traditions.

Given the wealth of New German Cinema literature that now exists, it is clearly impossible within this introductory study to offer a fully comprehensive overview and analysis of the cinema's origins. The aim in chapter 1 is rather to draw on a range of critical approaches with reference to the existing literature to explore some of the more significant historical, cultural, economic and institutional factors – namely the American dominance of the German market place, the development of a film subsidy system, the notion and politics of an *Autorenkino*, the framework of European art cinema, and distribution and exhibition initiatives – that helped facilitate the birth of and shape a new national cinema in West Germany.

The second question which structures this book is why did these films make such an impression on the international cinema scene, what did they achieve that the films of the 1950s failed to? The New German Cinema directors were certainly talented film-makers and a number of them had distinctive styles – something which contributed to the evaluation of the films as a 'cinéma des auteurs'. As Charles Eidsvik says of Herzog, for instance, in an early study:

> [He] links dream and reality, the grotesque and the normal, the bizarre and the everyday … Herzog puts extreme subjects into extreme situations in narratives structured like dreams … Perhaps excepting Bergman and Murnau, no film-maker has ever created visions as intense and disturbing as Herzog's. (1979: 169–70)

However, their films were also funded with public money, and deliberately promoted and exported as a 'quality' national cinema. By contrast, in the

1950s there was virtually no public funding available for film production, forcing directors to work in a commercial environment, and the resulting films have been characterised as 'drab', and even 'shoddy', by some critics.

But it is possible to argue that, more than anything, it was the films' engagement with contemporary West German reality that made them so significant, since it was a reality that seemed to have been consistently denied in the films of the 1950s. In Germany, dealing with contemporary reality often meant confronting the recent Nazi past – either obliquely or directly – a history that many preferred to forget but one that had so clearly influenced the present. Eric Rentschler has therefore characterised the films as 'the quest for alternative images and counter-representations' (1984: 4). Rather than offer a comprehensive overview of the thematic issues addressed by the New German Cinema, chapter 2 will examine a number of contemporary concerns that emerge across a range of films in order to explore some of those counter-representations: the presence of the *Gastarbeiter* in West Germany; the rise of urban terrorism in the 1970s; the 'remembering' of the experience of Nazism; the role of American cultural imperialism in shaping the experiences of the post-war generation, especially with regard to Hollywood cinema; and lastly, the development of the women's movement which had a powerful effect on West German society as a whole and hence on film-making too, where it addressed important questions about history and how we document it. The chapter will conclude by arguing that the counter-representations offered by many New German Cinema films raised important questions about West Germany's self-understanding and in fact constituted a series of counter-myths about German identity in the post-war era.

And lastly, what caused the New German Cinema's demise? It is possible to argue that, with the cinema's dependence on public funding, its existence from the outset was precarious and was indeed repeatedly threatened. As a whole network of film subsidies developed during the late 1960s and 1970s, it may have facilitated access to the means of production, but the requirements of the funding agencies also frequently constrained directors both creatively and politically. What started out as a challenging and formally innovative cinema gradually became a more mainstream and predominately realist narrative-based one. And at times avenues of funding became much reduced or even dried up altogether. Chapter 3 will therefore re-examine the film subsidy system that is detailed in chapter 1 to show how the New German Cinema was always at the mercy of changing institutional, economic and political conditions. Whilst its dependence on state initiatives gave rise to some imaginative approaches to film-making, it also meant that the new cinema was always faced with the possibility of its own demise.

Also, just as the directors have been attributed with bringing it into existence, they can similarly be seen as a cause of its demise. Fassbinder, by far the most prolific of the new film-makers, died in 1982, while other directors – like Herzog and Wenders – spent periods working abroad and for various reasons turned to non-German subject matter. But other factors also played an important role. In particular, by the 1980s the conditions of film funding and production had changed considerably at both the national and international levels and this impacted significantly on the kinds of films being made. Chapter 3 will examine these changed circumstances, the effects they had on film-making in West Germany, and how they gave rise to the perception that the era of the New German Cinema had come to an end.

1   ORIGINS: FROM 'AUTOR' TO AUDIENCES

The American legacy

New German Cinema is the term usually applied to a loose grouping of films that were made in West Germany during the 1960s, 1970s and early 1980s, and these films were deemed to mark the emergence of a new 'quality' national cinema. How did these films get made, and why were they regarded as a quality national cinema? Although the directors of these films were undoubtedly highly talented, there were a number of historically specific factors that set up some essential pre-conditions for the emergence of the New German Cinema.

One of the key factors was the way in which the Allies handled the fledging West German film industry in the years immediately after the Second World War. Guided by self-interest, their policies had a directly detrimental effect on German cinema which by the 1950s had become highly provincial, escapist and largely unsuitable for the export market. And it was the combination of individual, institutional and state responses to this situation that eventually precipitated the emergence of a new German cinema.

At the end of the war the Western Allies had felt it was vital to 're-educate' the German people in order both to 'denazify' Germany and to build up the Western zones of Germany as a buffer to the Soviet influence in eastern Europe. American films were quickly identified as an effective way of disseminating Western notions of freedom, democracy and capitalist enterprise. In a famous speech Spyros Skouras, head of Twentieth-Century Fox, declared that their films were a potential means of 'indoctrinating people into the free way of life and instil[ling] in them a compelling desire for freedom ... we as an industry can play an infinitely important part in the world-wide ideological struggle for the minds of men, and confound the Communist propagandists' (in Guback 1969: 125). However, American distributors were also keen to protect their economic interests and insisted that they should be allowed to transfer any profits made from the exhibition of their films in Germany back to America. Since the German market had been closed to America during the war, once this condition was met, Hollywood had an enormous backlog of films which had already gone into profit and could be made available at highly competitive prices. As a result American companies rapidly achieved a position of economic dominance in West Germany: by the beginning of the 1950s over two hundred American films were being released there each year.

Unsurprisingly, the American Motion Picture Export Association was keen to protect this lucrative new market. Measures were therefore taken to prevent the imposition of an import quota on American films – a safeguard introduced in other European countries after the war in order to protect their own film industries – which meant that American companies remained free to flood the German market with Hollywood films. The Allies also dismantled the remnants of the Nazi film industry which had been centralised and state controlled through a giant conglomerate, UFA. Decartelisation laws were passed which broke up UFA and separated out the various production, distribution and exhibition branches of the industry, and only small independent production companies were licensed. The aim was to permit an indigenous film industry to develop, but one that lacked the scale and economic power to threaten America's monopoly of the German market. And in this the Allies' policies were very successful.

Forced to remain small-scale and with production dispersed around the country, the German industry failed to attract any substantial investment. Moreover, as the country's economic recovery started to take off, other industries prospered and offered safer investment opportunities than the traditionally high-risk area of film production. Also, in countries like Britain and France, American distributors became investors in indigenous film production as their profits were frozen in those countries. But in West Germany, American companies had little incentive to invest in West German production as they could transfer any profits back to the USA. In an attempt to stimulate production the government introduced a system of guaranteed credits in 1950 to encourage producers to raise finance for film projects. But owing to its administrative unwieldiness – and despite modifications – the system proved unsuccessful and was withdrawn in the mid-1950s.

This overall lack of investment meant that German films had to be produced relatively cheaply, making them unable to compete with the expensively produced Hollywood spectacle. As a result, indigenous production was quickly directed towards catering expressly for German audiences and mostly comprised *Heimatfilme* – homeland films – which depicted simple country life in a rural Germany, adventure films based on popular German novels, historical films set in imperial Austria, together with romantic adventures and comedies set in picturesque locations. However, this overwhelming orientation towards the home market rendered German films on the whole unsuitable for export. This meant that films had to try and break even on national box-office receipts alone, which ensured production remained low-budget and resulted in a national cinema marked by correspondingly low production values. Compared with the Hollywood product, German films made in the 1950s looked decidedly drab and provincial and did little for the reputation of German cinema abroad. Thus, by the end of the 1950s the Allies' pursuit of their own political and economic interests had played a significant role in rendering West German cinema artistically impoverished and economically vulnerable.

Escaping reality

The films of the 1950s have also been characterised as 'escapist' – indeed, one foreign critic was moved to observe that in post-war West German

9

films the 'events of the 1930s and 1940s are either ignored or treated as something remote, regrettable, and faintly unmentionable, like halitosis or prostitution in Paraguay' (in Sandford 1981: 156). Although there were exceptions, this general trend is hardly surprising for a number of reasons. Under the Nazi regime, for instance, the film industry had been tightly controlled by the Ministry for Propaganda and Popular Enlightenment. Its head, Joseph Goebbels, had quickly identified the propaganda potential of cinema and had informed the industry that he wanted film to be used in support of the new regime. Gradually all film companies came under state control and by 1942 the whole industry had been centralised under UFA. Consequently, for many the cinema had been tainted by Nazism, and this bred a distrust of all but the most innocuous-seeming German films. Indeed, an early West German production, *Film without a Title* (*Film ohne Titel*, 1947) by Helmut Käutner, broached this very issue. A film about its own making, it addresses the question of how to make a film about the war. In it three directors discuss various versions of the story they want to tell, debating issues around film style and so on. But they also suggest that one of the problems concerning how to tell this particular story is that no film language is morally untainted and will thus have implications for the telling of the story.

Given the traumas and upheaval of the war, followed by the division of Germany which exiled many people from their families and former homes, it was also virtually inevitable that there would be audience demand for an 'escapist' cinema. The *Heimat* films in particular attracted viewers to the cinemas in record numbers. This in turn precipitated a brief boom for the industry during the mid-1950s with feature film production reaching an all-time high in 1955 with 122 productions and cinema attendance peaking the following year.

But perhaps more importantly, although UFA had been dismantled, denazification of the film industry workforce was virtually impossible. Most of the directors, writers, actors, cameramen and technicians had been members of the Nazi Party, but were nevertheless re-employed after the war. This was partly because those directors who had opposed the Nazi regime – such as Fritz Lang, Billy Wilder, Ernst Lubitsch and Douglas Sirk – had fled the country when the Nazis came to power.

But with the escalation of the Cold War, the recruitment of ex-Nazis was considered preferable to the risk of communist infiltration. Whilst critics have disagreed on the extent to which employees of the Nazi film industry were *active* party members, the fact remains that by 1960 over 40 per cent of working film directors had been prominent in Nazi cinema. Consequently, according to Helmut Herbst, the new West German film industry became a 'closed shop', largely controlled and run by the old UFA generation (1985: 70). Irrespective of the *actual* political leanings of the workforce, this continuity with the past severely limited the chance of the German cinema experiencing a cultural rebirth in the West after the war.

This was exacerbated by another factor. From 1955 quality ratings could be awarded to films which entitled the producer to considerable relief from entertainment tax. However, government representatives sat on the awards committees, and hence helped determine what constituted 'quality'. Unfortunately, this had the effect of discouraging film-makers from addressing 'difficult' subjects, such as the Nazi past, or adopting a critical stance on contemporary issues. As a result, 'it encouraged mediocrity and conformism, and the official list of "valuable" films for the 1950s reads more like a roll call of the world's worst movies than a guide to a nation's film culture' (Elsaesser 1989: 20).

There were a few notable exceptions: Bernard Wicki's *The Bridge* (*Die Brücke*, 1959), for instance, became a classic anti-war film, while Wolfgang Staudte's *Roses for the Prosecutor* (*Rosen für den Staatsanwalt*, 1959) addressed the fact that former Nazi officers had obtained positions of power in the new Federal Republic of Germany. But even films such as these could not prevent what became a steady decline in the international standing of West German film. As the 1950s progressed, production figures and box-office receipts also began to decline. By 1963 both had fallen by 50 per cent, and gradually cinemas started to close. Although other factors contributed to this decline of the film industry – such as the increase in car ownership – the advent of television (as elsewhere in Europe and the USA) played a significant role. Whereas in 1956 there had been fewer than 0.7 million televisions sets in West Germany, by 1963 this number had risen to 9 million.

The fight for survival

It had become apparent even in the mid-1950s that, if German cinema was to survive, government intervention would be necessary. Representatives from the industry began to lobby parliament and by the end of the 1950s criticism of West German cinema was being voiced from a number of quarters. In 1959 two young film-makers, Haro Senft and Ferdinand Khittl, campaigned to highlight the need to improve the quality of films and to provide grant aid for film projects. Two years later, in 1961, film critic Joe Hembus condemned the industry's 'factory-like production system where standardised models are turned out on an assembly-line' (quoted in Johnston 1979–80: 72). And in the same year the organisers of the Venice Film Festival rejected all the West German entries, while at home the Federal Film Prizes given annually by the Federal Ministry of the Interior (BMI) – often awarded to films exhibiting an anti-communist and pro-NATO stance yet also intended to celebrate 'quality' – went unawarded for best feature film, best director and best screenplay.

In February 1962 a group of 26 film-makers, writers and artists, spearheaded by Alexander Kluge and including Khittl and Senft, added their voices to this mounting condemnation of West German film. They drew up the Oberhausen Manifesto – so named because it was published during that year's Oberhausen Short Film Festival. In it they argued that given the opportunity they could create a 'new German feature film' which would replace the – for them – obviously defunct 'papa's cinema':

> The collapse of the conventional German film finally removes the economic justification from a mentality which we reject. The new German film thereby has a chance of coming to life.
>
> In recent years German short films by young authors, directors and producers have received a large number of prizes at international festivals and have won international critical acclaim. These works and their success shows that the future of the German film lies with those who have demonstrated that they speak a new film language.
>
> In Germany, as in other countries, the short film has become a training ground and arena of experimentation for the feature film.

We declare our right to create the new German feature film.

This new film needs new freedoms. Freedom from the usual conventions of the industry. Freedom from the influence of commercial partners. Freedom from the tutelage of other groups with vested interests.

We have concrete ideas about the production of the new German film with regard to its intellectual, formal and economic aspects. We are collectively prepared to take economic risks.

The old film is dead. We believe in the new.

In declaring 'The old film is dead', the signatories were in fact being rather presumptuous. Although production figures and box-office receipts had fallen, the industry had not entirely collapsed, as they would soon discover. However, their demands, combined with the accumulation of critical voices, struck a chord and prompted the government into action. Two months later, in April, the government announced plans to launch a new scheme to provide grants for feature film projects, scripts and script outlines. It took three years before a film subsidy agency – the *Kuratorium junger deutscher Film* (Board of Young German Film) – was actually set up but, launched in October 1965 and funded by the BMI, the Kuratorium was given a brief to promote the kind of film-making demanded by the Oberhausen Manifesto signatories and to 'stimulate a renewal of the German film in a manner exclusively and directly beneficial to the community' (quoted in Dawson 1981: 16). The BMI granted DM5 million to finance the Kuratorium's first three years of operation, and a selection committee composed largely of film critics and journalists was elected to allocate the money. The funding took the form of interest-free production loans of up to DM300,000 for *first* feature films only. Such an avenue of funding – not entirely dependent on commercial criteria – was of real significance, since it is the transition from short film-making (be that documentary, experimental or narrative) to full-length feature film-making that can be the most difficult to make, because of the latter's far higher production costs. Hence it meant that for the first time new, young film-makers who had been unable to gain access to the commercial film industry had a real chance to break into feature film production. The loans were to be repayable from box-office receipts, and the repayments would create a self-sustaining fund which could be used to finance further film production.

Initially the Kuratorium was very successful in fulfilling its brief. Within two years twenty-five films had been produced with Kuratorium funding, including Kluge's own first feature, *Yesterday Girl* (*Abschied von gestern*, 1965–66). A further three were by fellow Oberhausen signatories Hans Jürgen Pohland (*Cat and Mouse/Katz und Maus*, 1966), Edgar Reitz (*Mealtimes/Mahlzeiten*, 1966), and Haro Senft (*The Gentle Course/Der sanfte Lauf*, 1967); and two more in this first batch of films were produced by signatory Rob Houwer. In direct contrast to the commercial industry, the contractual arrangements governing the Kuratorium loans allowed film-makers to retain a high degree of artistic control. As a result most of these films broke with the formal conventions of mainstream cinema, varying from episodic and experimental narratives to highly avant-garde pieces. They also dealt with contemporary concerns in a way that contrasted sharply and refreshingly with the 'escapist' nature of 1950s German cinema, and seemed indeed to have brought to life a new kind of German film.

This marrying of contemporary issues with formal experimentation is particularly evident in Kluge's *Yesterday Girl*. Made in black and white, the film is based on the real-life story of a young Jewish woman, Anita G, who comes to West Germany (Federal Republic of Germany) at the end of the 1950s from what was then East Germany (German Democratic Republic) in an attempt to make a new life for herself. In a highly episodic and impressionistic narrative, the film follows Anita through a number of unsuccessful jobs, an attempt to further her education, a couple of attempts to steal, and a series of unhappy affairs which end with her becoming pregnant by a government official called Pichota. Unable to support herself financially, she sleeps rough and wanders the streets with her suitcase. Finally she turns herself over to the police and has her baby in prison.

Kluge's film-making can probably be best described as 'Brechtian' (and his films have also been compared to those of French New Wave director Jean-Luc Godard). As in Brecht's epic theatre, Kluge's films use a

FIGURE 1 Alexandra Kluge as Anita G in *Yesterday Girl* (1965–66)

number of formal devices to discourage viewers from identifying with the fictional characters, to challenge people's usual forms of perception, and to stimulate a questioning attitude towards their surroundings rather than provide reassurance.

For instance, Kluge incorporates a number of intertitles in the film, which seem to either unnecessarily mark particular points in the narrative – 'One day in the Manager's absence, Anita is dismissed', 'Pichota, Under-Secretary awaits his ministerial colleagues' and 'She wants to start a new life' – or offer more general and often unexplained reflections on life – 'Will yesterday come tomorrow?', 'Truth is killed when it really appears' and 'I know a miracle will happen one day'. Knowledge of silent and mainstream film conventions leads the viewer to expect these intertitles to further the narrative or structure the film's temporality, but instead they are incidental comments which arbitrarily segment it, disrupting the narrative flow and foregrounding the film's construction. Indeed, although the film has a fairly contemporary setting, the time span of the events depicted is never made clear – as viewers we have no idea how long Anita stays in jobs or how long her affairs last.

Kluge also eschews other mainstream film conventions, such as shot-reverse-shot and the use of establishing shots. One scene in the film, for instance, commences by alternating between frontal close-ups of a young man and of Anita. Without the conventional opening establishing shot, the viewer has no idea of where the two characters are in relation to one another, or even if they are 'together'. On other occasions, Kluge uses panning shots between two characters or speeded-up footage of action in long shot, which draw attention to the presence of the camera. Verbal commentary, documentary-style direct address to camera by some characters and old photos are also intercut which both illustrate and invite reflection upon the narrative sequences.

And the events that constitute Anita's story are often only shown obliquely – we see only the court proceedings against Anita that result from a theft, not the theft itself, nor where it took place or its discovery. In some cases we are given only a brief indication that Anita is having an affair – a short scene, for instance, of her being intimate with someone in her flat – not how, why or where it started. The only indication of Anita's pregnancy is a scene of her in a public toilet taking a urine sample and a brief conversation with Pichota where he advises her to go to North Rhine-Westfalia and gives her DM100. The actual fact of the pregnancy is never mentioned, leaving the viewer to deduce that Pichota is suggesting and giving Anita money for an abortion. Similarly, in prison no mention is made of her impending motherhood and, although we briefly see her in labour, we never see the baby.

These formal devices give the film a very disjointed feel, something that is compounded by the use of music on the soundtrack which is often inappropriate to the visual images it accompanies – the scenes of Anita wandering the streets towards the end of the film, for instance, are accompanied by very upbeat and lively music. They also draw attention to the film as a construct and prevent the viewer from being drawn into the fictional world or identifying too closely with Anita. This means the viewer has to take a very active role in constructing the film's meaning – indeed, Sandford reports that on its release some critics confessed to finding the film 'not a little perplexing' (1981: 22) – but it can precipitate a more analytical consideration of the issues and ideas raised by *Yesterday Girl*.

The German title of the film translates literally as 'taking leave of yesterday', which suggests that through the figure of Anita and her flight to West Germany the film is highlighting a desire to escape the past. This is made overt in the opening sequence of the film, when a judge who is trying Anita for the theft of a colleague's cardigan questions her about her Jewish parentage and then declares 'it's past, let's forget it'. But as a Jew who leaves the GDR, she acts as a reminder both of the Nazi persecution of the Jews and of the communist rejection of capitalism. Thus, through the character of Anita the film links together questions of German history and the contemporary situation of post-war divided Germany, suggesting the inseparability of past and present. This is reinforced by the fact that Anita fails miserably to make a new life for herself. She loses her job selling foreign language course records, for instance, because her boss's wife thinks he is having an affair with her, the University won't let her register to study because she does not have a school leaving certificate, she has to leave her lodgings because she cannot pay her rent, and she cannot become Pichota's wife because he is already married. She even makes the pretence of starting a new life by taking Pichota to see a flat on which she says she has put a deposit, but he knows she cannot afford it. Just as she would have failed to fit into Nazi Germany and has failed to fit into East Germany, so she fails time and again to integrate into the Federal Republic:

she cannot escape her past and will remain 'an unwanted outsider' (Sandford 1981: 21). Her specific situation is, of course, peculiarly German, and thus Kluge's film can be understood as a film about Germany, one that suggests that while people may wish to forget the Nazi past and may feel they have made a break with it, it nevertheless is and will remain an essential precondition of and for understanding the present socio-political situation.

In addition to their engagement with contemporary concerns, a number of these first Kuratorium-funded films also enjoyed unprecedented critical acclaim. In addition to the Special Jury Prize at the 1966 Venice Film Festival, Kluge's film won the Film Award in Gold in several categories – including Outstanding Feature Film – at the Federal Film Awards the following year. In particular, Kluge's sister Alexandra who played Anita G was acclaimed for her performance, 'the best the post-war German cinema had seen' (Sandford 1981: 21). According to Sandford, when the film was shown at Venice critics voted her the 'most outstanding female player', surpassing Julie Christie and Jane Fonda (*ibid.*). And in 1967 Edgar Reitz's *Mealtimes* (*Mahlzeiten*, 1966) received the Best First Work award at Venice. This success also seemed to mark the beginning of a new phase in West German cinema generally. Non-Kuratorium financed films by other new directors were well received at Cannes in 1966, especially Ulrich Schamoni's *It* (*Es*, 1965), Volker Schlöndorff's *Young Törless* (*Der junge Törless,* 1966), and Jean-Marie Straub and Danièle Huillet's *Not Reconciled* (*Nicht versöhnt*, 1965). Back in Germany Peter Schamoni's *Closed Season for Foxes* (*Schonzeit für Füchse*, 1966) won a Silver Bear at the Berlin Film Festival; and between 1967 and 1969 two more Kuratorium films (in addition to Kluge's *Yesterday Girl*) and three further films by new young directors also won Federal Film Prizes. Moreover, recognition that something was happening on the West German film scene went beyond the film festival committees. According to Reitz:

> The press was unbelievably positive. And when the first films came out, there was a degree of public interest which has never been matched since. Films like *Abschied von gestern*, or my own *Mahlzeiten*, attracted audiences of over a million. (in Dawson 1981: 17)

Consequently, the setting up of the Kuratorium and this first batch of critically acclaimed films appeared to many observers to have indeed brought about 'a renewal of the German film', to have produced the new quality national cinema implicitly called for in the Oberhausen Manifesto. And this point is often taken to mark the start of what became termed the Young German Film – a phenomenon which subsequently matured into the New German Cinema – although a whole set of historically specific circumstances had set the essential pre-conditions for its emergence.

The development of a film subsidy network

However, the Young German Film – for all its critical acclaim – was very nearly an extremely short-lived phenomenon. Having made their first feature films, the new directors became ineligible for further Kuratorium funding and were faced with limited possibilities for financing subsequent films. If they had failed to win a Federal Film Prize which carried a cash award for future production work, they had to turn to the diminishing commercial sources. Furthermore, although the first batch of Kuratorium films had been well received, they did not do well enough in the cinemas to fully repay their loans, leaving the subsidy agency with rapidly diminishing funds.

At the same time the commercial sector viewed Kuratorium-funded films as unfair competition. In a market where it was increasingly difficult to produce films on a commercial basis, it seemed as if young film-makers were being given money to make whatever films they liked. As Joe Hembus commented in January 1966:

In this same German cinema where the emergence of a *single* new film-maker used to create quite a sensation, the first works of no fewer than six film-makers have made their debut since October 1965. In the upcoming months there will be at least six more. If that continues, we'll see more films by new film-makers than by the old in 1966. (in Phillips 1984: xvii)

Unsurprisingly the film industry started to lobby the German government, demanding that any film subsidies should be directed towards revitalising the commercial sector, and was successful in bringing about a more commercially orientated revision of film policy. In December 1967 a new Film Development Act (the FFG) was passed which raised a levy on every cinema ticket sold in West Germany to provide funding (estimated to amount to DM15 million) for film production, and the Film Development Board (the FFA) was set up to administer these funds. In complete contrast to the Kuratorium's support for first-time feature film directors, FFA funding was awarded to film projects on the basis of the financial success of the producer's previous film. As long as it had grossed DM500,000, or DM300,000 if it had been awarded a quality rating, during the first two years of its release, a production subsidy for the producer's next film was automatically awarded. The criteria were later changed to minimum audience attendance figures, but the principle of automatic subsidy linked to previous box-office performance remained.

Consequently, first time directors were ineligible for FFA funding, and most of the new films had not done well enough at the box-office to trigger the FFA funding mechanism. Distributors also started to withdraw films by new directors like Kluge and Reitz and replace them with industry fare, so that the commercial sector could monopolise the new subsidy money. After the FFG had been passed, the BMI also ceased funding the Kuratorium and passed responsibility down to regional government. In 1969 the individual federal states agreed to provide the agency with an annual budget of DM750,000, which constituted more than a 50 per cent reduction in its resources and resulted in the funding of correspondingly fewer films. As a result, by the early 1970s the Young German Film appeared to be on the verge of disappearing, while the commercial sector cashed in on the new source of film subsidy.

However, it also soon became apparent that the FFG was actually failing to stimulate the economic revival of the industry. The retroactive nature of the FFA funding encouraged producers to go for tried and tested formula films, resulting in a plethora of sex films, low-brow classroom comedies and the like, a cinema of 'unparalleled mediocrity' as one observer described it (Phillips 1984: xviii). This in turn drove significant segments of the cinema audience away and led to further cinema closures. Indeed, as early as 1968 the federal parliament resolved that the commercial basis of the film policy revisions had to be supplemented by cultural funding aimed at, among other things, raising quality standards and ensuring support for new young film-makers. Although this was signalled as a priority, it took several years to adequately revise the FFG. And in the short term it was in fact television that ensured the continuing existence of Germany's promising new cinema – an ironic turn of events, given that it had been television which had contributed so significantly to the decline in cinema audiences.

At the time there were ten broadcasting companies in West Germany – nine regional ones which constituted the national network of the first channel (ARD) and the regional networks of the third channel, and *Zweites Deutsches Fernsehen* (ZDF) which broadcast the second national channel. These were public corporations and produced relatively few programmes themselves, commissioning commercial companies or freelance independents to produce the rest – providing in fact the model for Channel 4 in Britain. Consequently, television represented an enormous source of potential funding for the new directors which they had started to tap as early as the late 1960s, and by the early 1970s they were increasingly turning to television companies to finance their film projects. Moreover, the corporations had a constitutional commitment to promoting cultural 'quality' and were likely to provide a more sympathetic producer than the film-makers would find in the commercial film industry. Just as importantly, in some cases, key personnel at the television stations also had a background in film and were highly supportive of the emerging new cinema. *Westdeutscher Rundfunk* (WDR), the Cologne television station, for instance, spawned a whole genre of critically acclaimed *Arbeiterfilme* (worker films) made by Erika Runge (*Why is Mrs B. Happy?/Warum ist Frau B. glücklich*, 1968), Helma Sanders-Brahms (*The White-Collar Worker/Der Angestellte*, 1971), Christian Ziewer (*Dear Mother, I'm OK/Liebe Mutter, mir geht es gut*, 1971), Fassbinder (*Eight Hours are not a Day/Acht Stunden sind kein Tag*, 1972) and others, which focused on the lives and experiences of the contemporary German working classes. Indeed, Fassbinder developed a long relationship with WDR, making a number of other television films and series for the station as well.

However, commissioning policies were fairly arbitrary and the contractual arrangements the television companies made with the film-makers were of a rather ad hoc nature. Being premiered on television also diminishes a film's prospects in the cinema – they tend not to do well at the box-office and hence commercial distributors are usually not interested in taking them on. After its broadcast, therefore, a director's film could become buried in the archives of a television company with little or no chance of further screenings.

To improve this overall situation, the role of television in West German cinema was formalised and regulated in 1974 via a Film and Television Agreement between the FFA and the ARD and ZDF television networks. The agreement committed the television corporations to providing DM34 million over a five-year period for film production. Productions funded by this scheme were guaranteed a cinema release before being broadcast on television, and further funds were given to the FFA to fund the development of film projects with no guarantee that television would be a co-producer of those projects. And as the 1970s progressed, television began to assume an increasingly important role in supporting and sustaining the new cinema. By the end of the decade, very few films were being made without television funding.

At the same time, the film subsidy system was also expanded and developed, gradually improving the funding options available. As the shortcomings of the FFG became apparent, the act underwent successive revisions which, for instance, ensured that pornographic and 'low-quality' films could not qualify for subsidies and permitted the FFA to make discretionary cash awards to 'good entertainment' films which had fulfilled certain audience attendance criteria. The Board also introduced project funding which could be awarded to any project that seemed likely 'to improve the quality and profitability of the German film' (quoted in Pflaum and Prinzler 1983: 99), irrespective of a producer's previous work. In 1977 the individual federal states who had taken over responsibility for the Kuratorium agreed to increase its funding. And in the same year the city of Berlin pioneered the idea of regional funding, which was designed both to encourage film-makers to bring work to that region and to promote productions of particular cultural and political interest to the city. Over the next four years Bavaria, Hamburg and North Rhine-Westphalia also introduced regional funding schemes. Although the Bavarian scheme was largely based on economic criteria, those of Hamburg and North Rhine-Westphalia had an explicit cultural orientation and were administered largely by the film-makers themselves.

As such revisions to the film subsidy system during the 1970s, particularly the formalising of television's role, began to substantially improve production opportunities, the Young German Film matured into the New German Cinema and began to reassert itself. As Elsaesser observes:

> Alongside films with an international art cinema appeal, which retained a prestige currency for German films abroad and fed back into the home market as successful international releases, films began to appear which were clearly more directly aimed at various chapters of the national television audience. Political questions, social issues, current affairs and historical topics began to be treated in fiction films and documentaries in a manner unknown before in the Federal Republic. (1989: 34)

By 1977–78 half of the feature films being made were deemed to belong to the new cinema and were winning renewed acclaim for German cinema. Among those that attracted particular attention were Volker Schlöndorff and Margarethe von Trotta's *The Lost Honour of Katharina Blum* (*Die verlorene Ehre der Katharina Blum*, 1975), Wenders' *Kings of the Road* (*Im Lauf der Zeit*, 1976), Hans-Jürgen Syberberg's *Hitler, A Film From Germany* (*Hitler – ein Film aus Deutschland*, 1976–77), von Trotta's *The Second Awakening of Christa Klages* (*Das zweite Erwachen der Christa Klages*, 1977), Fassbinder's *The Marriage of Maria Braun* (*Die Ehe der Maria Braun*, 1978), and Schlöndorff's *The Tin Drum* (*Die Blechtrommel*, 1979).

Thus, the criticism of West German cinema in the late 1950s and early 1960s eventually precipitated the development of a whole system of public subsidies. Whilst the subsidy system was not without its problems – something which will be explored in chapter 3 – it nevertheless helped consolidate the emergence of a critically acclaimed new cinema by the end of the 1970s. Taken together, this complex network of film subsidies can be understood at one level as a much needed institutional initiative designed to promote and develop a national cinema that was on the one hand culturally motivated, yet at the same time economically viable. However, laudable though such aims were, the subsidy system was not entirely successful in combining them. Writing in 1981, Olga Grüber asserted that 'Of the approximately 300 productions that could be counted as "New German Cinema" about six were commercially successful in German cinemas and just about broke even' (quoted in Elsaesser 1989: 37). One of those fortunate few was Schlöndorff's *The Tin Drum*.

Schlöndorff's film is an adaptation of the first two parts of Günter Grass' novel *The Tin Drum*. Grass had been a relatively unknown writer, but on its publication in 1959 *The Tin Drum* sold over 300,000 copies in Germany, nearly half a million in translation in the US, and was hailed as a masterpiece. With the book enjoying numerous reprints, Grass had been approached many times with proposals for its filming but held out until he found an acceptable script and eventually worked with the scriptwriters on Schlöndorff's film. Hence, even before its release, the film benefited from strong literary credentials and a potentially sizeable audience of people already familiar with, or at least aware of, the book and Grass' reputation. The film focuses on Oskar Matzerath, whose colourful life is interwoven with the political fate of Danzig and its Polish, Jewish and German populations during the 1920s and the subsequent Nazi era. The film starts by relating Oskar's pre-history, from when his grandmother conceives his mother, Agnes, in 1899, through Agnes' love for her Polish cousin Jan and marriage to Alfred, to Oskar's birth in 1924. It then follows Oskar through his childhood into adulthood at the end of the Second World War when he is twenty.

Although Schlöndorff has described the film as series of 'tableaux' (quoted in Sandford 1981: 47), its narrative form is in fact more conventional and hence far more accessible to a wider audience than Kluge's *Yesterday Girl*, with the passing of time clearly marked by historical events, occasional dates and Oskar's age. While rooted in historical reality, the content nevertheless incorporates fantastical elements. On his third birthday, for instance, Oskar is given a tin drum by his mother through which he discovers an ability to shatter glass objects when he screams, a talent which he uses to exercise a degree of control over his life. More

FIGURE 2 David Bennett as the 3-year-old Oskar in *The Tin Drum* (1979)

importantly, at the age of three, due to the moral and political corruption that he has witnessed in the adult world, Oskar decides to stop growing and remains child-like in stature throughout the film. A potentially impossible element of the book to reproduce filmically, the role is beautifully brought to life through a mesmerising performance by David Bennett, a 12-year-old boy with large entrancing eyes who had the physique of a much younger child. Bennent's performance was repeatedly acclaimed by critics and was undoubtedly a contributing factor to the film's success. As Geoff Brown asserted, for instance: 'All meanings are centred on the hero and here Schlöndorff has been spectacularly fortunate, for the performance of the 12-year-old David Bennent is one of great force' (Brown 1980).

The use of a child figure as the central protagonist allows the film to represent historical events from an intriguing 'alternative' perspective. We are presented with and invited to adopt Oskar's viewpoint – even at his birth, which is filmed from his perspective as he emerges from his mother's womb into the awaiting world. The camera is repeatedly positioned at Oskar's eye level, looking up at the adult world or out at it from a hiding place, so that we are forced to look at the world from Oskar's three-year-old perspective. Through this formal device Oskar is shown to see things that the adults only suspect or choose to ignore – such as his mother's infidelity with her cousin Jan, or the regimented indoctrination of Nazi party members like his German father Alfred. And this perspective is reinforced by Oskar's voice-over narration throughout the film offering his interpretation of events. His child's view of the world locates personal experience – such as his mother Agnes, torn between her Polish cousin and her German husband; or a Jewish toyshop owner declaring his love to Agnes; or Oskar's first love, Maria, who comes to housekeep for them after his mother's death – as caught up in the wider reality of Nazi politics and the outbreak of war. It is clearly represented as a subjective view, but also a privileged one as Oskar goes unnoticed by the adults he observes. It reveals a less pleasant side to human nature, and offers a stinging and detached yet often humorous and poignant critique of the interplay between historical events and human emotions.

Not only did the film win the Academy Award for Best Foreign Language Film in 1980, it also won several other awards both at home and abroad, including the Palme d'Or at the 1979 Cannes Film Festival. Time and again reviewers noted Grass' collaboration on the film as an assurance of cultural quality, while congratulating Schlöndorff on transforming Grass' – at times – heavy prose into an intelligent and imaginative, yet accessible film.[1] While financial success does not always go hand in hand with such critical acclaim, *The Tin Drum* was watched by over 900,000 viewers within eight months of being released in Germany. This contrasted dramatically with the attendance figures for films by other New German Cinema directors, such as Kluge, Helma Sanders-Brahms, Werner Schroeter and Helke Sander, which frequently attracted fewer than 150,000 viewers.

As the case of *The Tin Drum* demonstrates, it is clearly possible to combine cultural 'quality' with accessibility for a wider audience, to achieve critical acclaim as well as (relative) economic success. But as Grüber asserts, the film was one of only a handful of exceptions. On the whole the new German cinema, while undoubtedly culturally motivated, never became an economically viable one. And even though it was promoted as a 'quality' national cinema, it is possible to argue – as a number of film-makers did – that even in this respect, the subsidy system was only a qualified success.

The Autorenkino

In order to promote the cultural 'quality' of the new cinema, the philosophy behind much of the subsidy system – despite the concern with economic viability – deliberately promoted a mode of production that is more usually associated with the arts: that is, one that recognises individual authorship and creativity. But this did not come about without prompting. It was partly a result of the deliberate and self-conscious promotion of the concept of an *Autorenkino* – a cinema of auteurs – by the film-makers themselves. Like the French concept of *auteur*, the German notion of *Autor* identifies the director as a film's creator and the film itself is regarded as an expression of that creator's personality.

Although he also placed important emphasis on the role of the viewer in creating meaning, Alexander Kluge was initially the chief exponent of an *Autorenkino* and promoted the notion in both his writings and campaigning work. This approach to cinema was already evident – unsurprisingly given Kluge's involvement – in the Oberhausen Manifesto: since the signatories insisted on freedom from economic and vested interests, they were basically opposing industrial modes of production and demanding the freedom of expression normally associated with 'artistic' production. In subsequent writings, Kluge developed the idea of the director as *Autor* by contrasting the new German film with what he termed a *Zutatenfilm* – a 'recipe film'. The 'recipe film' was a typical industry product, made up of ingredients such as stars, ideas, directors, technicians and scriptwriters which the producer simply went out and purchased according to requirements. In contrast, the new directors would bring something personal to their films, making the new German film more than just the sum of its parts.

During the 1960s Kluge developed these ideas, together with Edgar Reitz, into a coherent education programme at a private college in Ulm. They developed a four-year course which offered students an all-round film education, familiarising them with all areas of production. Instead of becoming specialists trained in a particular area, such as camera, editing or direction, in readiness for an industrial context, students would become *Filmautoren* – that is, directors who exercised a far greater degree of authorial control than industrial production methods normally permitted and who could consequently use film as a medium for personal expression. This avenue of training was the first of its kind in the Federal Republic, but when the German Film and Television Academy in Berlin (DFFB) opened in 1966 it adopted a similar approach, stating that its training goal was

> to provide future film-makers who want to work independently with a theoretical and practical basis for their later professional activity. It is not divided into specialist areas, but offers a unified training programme. (Pflaum and Prinzler 1979: 85)

In large part due to the lobbying efforts of Kluge and others, the demands of the Oberhausen Manifesto and the concept of an *Autorenkino* directly informed the guidelines drawn up for the Kuratorium. In his account of its work, Hermann Gerber explains that 'according to the fundamental Oberhausen principle the film-maker was to have autonomy in giving shape to his film idea ... he was to retain control over the direction and entire production process' (1977: 7). Thus the Kuratorium clearly identified the director as a film's author and endeavoured to guarantee his or her independence, implying that film-making is an act of personal expression and hence an art form. Indeed, the Kuratorium was modelled on forms of patronage and commission that had traditionally supported the fine arts. Hence, unlike the French concept of 'auteur' which was applied to a director retrospectively on the basis of an existing oeuvre of work, the status of *Autor* was conferred on the film-makers both conceptually and institutionally *before* they had even made their first films.

Over the years the directors associated with the New German Cinema continued to promote film as an art form and themselves as *Autoren*. In interviews they frequently made statements which served to reinforce the idea of themselves as gifted auteurs. In 1978, for instance, Fassbinder declared in an interview for *Time*: 'We had nothing, and we started with nothing ... For a generation nobody made important films in Germany.

Until us' (Clarke 1978: 51). That they were likely to push for as much authorial legitimation as possible is not surprising since it enhanced their personal prestige and institutional power. Indeed, Thomas Elsaesser argues that 'the fact that they expressed views and took positions publicly became an integral part of being film-makers' (1989: 75). And others, like *Basis Film*, for instance, also took up the notion of an *Autorenkino*. As an independent producer and distributor of new German films, Basis identified the *Autorenfilm* as essential to the survival of a national film culture and stressed the need to 'fight for the recognition of film as cultural property ... with an author whose rights must be protected and whose artistic freedom is inalienable' (Burckner 1987: II/2–3). And the company specifically structured their production and distribution policies to support and maintain the existence of an *Autorenkino*, asserting that 'all essential decisions are the responsibility ... exclusively of the film-maker' (*ibid.*).

This take up of the *Autorenkino* principle and its institutional sanctioning by the Kuratorium was not, however, due *solely* to the efforts of Kluge and his colleagues. Their campaigning coincided with a political will to use film as a means of promoting and exporting German culture as a manifestation of national identity, particularly to counter any rival claims on 'German' culture made by the GDR – a central ideological tenet of the Federal Republic was that West Germany should be the sole legitimate representative of German culture and German history. To target the overseas markets the West German government vigorously promoted the New German Cinema through its embassies and Goethe Institutes and actively supported the cinema's 'top talents' as their cultural ambassadors. While the film subsidy system was undeniably shaped by economic considerations, it was equally determined therefore by a politically motivated argument that film – like literature, theatre, music and the fine arts – should be regarded as an autonomous art form. And as the subsidy system evolved, most of the agencies followed the Kuratorium's lead and identified the director as a film's author. Thus the concept of an *Autorenkino* played an important political role in creating a space for film production outside of the commercial mainstream.

The concrete result of all this was that the contractual arrangements between the funding bodies and directors encouraged film-makers to assume a greater responsibility and to take on more than just the directorial role – something which helped critics abroad to see the films as a 'cinéma des auteurs'. Film-makers often became their own scriptwriters and/or producers as well as taking many of the artistic, casting, editing and organisational decisions. Although the importance and tenability of the *Autorenkino* concept declined in the latter half of the 1970s, film-makers were – to start with – seemingly in a position to exercise a large degree of creative control over their films.

In some ways, however, this was a mixed blessing. In reality it encouraged the development of a small, team-based 'cottage industry' – where film-making became more like practising a craft than engaging in a technological process. This nevertheless helped give the cinema a clearly identifiable character, but one somewhat at odds with the notion of an *Autorenkino*. Compared to the size of investment normally associated with film production in the commercial sector or even the 'quality' art-house cinema, the loans and subsidies granted by the various film promotion agencies were usually extremely small. During the 1970s film-makers were often producing feature films for between DM80,000 and DM200,000 while Italian or French directors in a similar situation might be working with budgets of at least DM800,000. When it was first set up, the *maximum* loan the Kuratorium could offer was DM300,000. These low levels of funding meant that directors were more or less forced to compromise with shorter shooting schedules and to employ absolute minimal production crews or work with non-professionals. In discussing her filming of *The Wolf Girl* (*Die Wolfsbraut*, 1985) Dagmar Beiersdorf explained the kinds of pressure that result when working under such conditions:

We were a small team of six people. No production manager, no extra people for make-up or costume. So, one is, of course, responsible for the bulk of the work oneself. For instance, I needed a piano for three days, but had no properties manager. So during filming I had to keep running to the phone in order to organize a van and a piano. Everywhere I was getting refusals because I couldn't pay the prices. And when I eventually got something agreed, it was 'but you have to collect and load yourself'. So at five o'clock in the morning – filming the piano scene was supposed to begin at nine – I set off, collected the van, picked up two sleepy friends, we drove out to Gatow and heaved the monstor into the bus. When we unloaded the thing again where we were filming shortly before nine o'clock, we were of course completely worn out. (in Knight 1992: 47)

Thus, as a contemporary writer observed: 'It is like trying to build a Rolls-Royce with money that is just enough to put together a bicycle' (in Elsaesser 1989: 25). However, for all its problems, working in small teams also allowed the development of much closer collaborations, and in fact the new film-makers frequently worked with the same people time and again. Wenders often collaborated with writer Peter Handke, actor Rüdiger Vogler and cameraman Robby Müller, Fassbinder with actress Hanna Schygulla, editors Thea Eymèsz and Juliane Lorenz, and cameramen Michael Ballhaus and Xaver Schwarzenberger, and both Herzog and Kluge with editor Beate Mainka-Jellinghaus, while Margarethe von Trotta either co-wrote, co-directed and/or acted in many films made by her then husband Volker Schlöndorff, and Jean-Marie Straub and Danièle Huillet always worked as a film-making team. A significant number of the directors also drew repeatedly on the same small pool of actors – especially Rüdiger Vogler, Hanna Schygulla, Angela Winkler, Bruno Ganz, Irm Hermann, Barbara Sukowa, Klaus Kinski and Eva Mattes – so much so that these actors virtually became the recognisable public face of the New German Cinema. Moreover, the new directors often acted in their own and each other's films. Hence it is in fact possible to argue that the apparently distinctive directorial styles owe as much to the recurring collaborative teamwork that characterises the production conditions of New German Cinema as they do to the promotion of and institutional support for an *Autorenkino*.

Unsurprisingly, the film-makers argued they needed larger subsidies if they were to produce a 'quality' national cinema, but the artisanal and team-based mode of production allowed a far greater degree of experimentation to take place than would have been possible in a conventional commercial context. Indeed, to a certain extent, such experimentation arose out of necessity. Although – as the Oberhausen Manifesto declared – many film-makers *wanted* to break with the 'old cinema' and to develop a new film language, small budgets meant it was actually impossible to make feature films according to the conventions of commercial cinema. Therefore, rather than trying to produce pale imitations, film-makers were in a sense *forced* to try and find completely different ways of working. Straub and Huillet's *Not Reconciled* (1965), for instance, which is based on a Heinrich Böll novel entitled *Billiards at Half Past Nine*, completely does away with the book's chronology and instead intermeshes simultaneously the present, the Nazi era and that of the First World War. Indeed, the publishers of Böll's novel tried to prevent the distribution and exhibition of the film 'on the grounds that the Straubs had unconscionably butchered the [original]' (Franklin 1983: 82). And some of the early films have been characterised by the way they seem to operate 'outside any recognisable tradition of film-making either commercial or avant-garde' (Elsaesser 1989: 25). While this freedom to experiment stemmed as much from necessity as from choice, it has of course contributed to the enormous stylistic and thematic diversity of the New German Cinema films.

European art cinema

However, such freedom to experiment and the notion of an *Autorenkino*, with its high level of directorial control, were not peculiar to West German film culture. While the New German Cinema was a product of specifically national conditions, in many ways it can also be viewed as part of the wider phenomenon of European art cinema. There is no precise definition of 'art cinema' as such, although it has been described in terms of its institutional base (Neale 1981) on the one hand and its narrational mode and aesthetic qualities (Bordwell 1985) on the other. Broadly speaking, it is usually identified as an area of film-making undertaken in various European countries both to counter American domination of their indigenous film markets and to nurture a film industry and culture of their own. It is also the area of film-making that usually gets exported and hence one that is often deemed to constitute a country's national cinema when viewed abroad, but in fact usually exists alongside a country's more popular and mainstream indigenous cinema. Reflecting on developments during the first part of the twentieth century, Léon Moussinac summed up the perceived importance of such film-making, although his specific concern was with the French cinema: 'In 1914, 90 per cent of the films shown throughout the world were French: by 1928, 85 per cent of them were American' (in Neale 1981: 16). Unsurprisingly, art cinema has therefore frequently – if inadequately – been defined in opposition to Hollywood cinema. As Paul Schrader has asserted, for instance:

> American movies are based on the assumption that life presents you with problems, while European [art] films are based on the conviction that life confronts you with dilemmas – and while problems are something you solve, dilemmas cannot be solved, they're merely probed or investigated. (in Elsaesser 1994: 24)

Broadly speaking, interest in 'film as art' generally started to develop in Europe after the First World War, often with the setting up of film clubs to show foreign films (especially from the USSR, such as those by Sergei Eisenstein and Dziga Vertov), with artists becoming involved in avant-garde film-making, and the appearance of books and magazines devoted to the 'art' of cinema, combined with the introduction of some state support for indigenous film industries. With the increased presence of the US generally and Hollywood films in particular in Europe after the Second World War, state support gradually became more firmly linked to the development and promotion of specifically *national* art cinemas, which often generated their own distribution and exhibition networks. The less overtly commercial nature of such cinemas usually afforded its directors a greater degree of control over their film-making, allowing them to be perceived as 'auteurs' – as was the case with New German Cinema. At the same time, especially during the 1950s, a new audience for film began emerging: college-educated, middle-class cinephiles looking for films of contemporary relevance. Such audiences sprang up across Europe, offering the various national art cinemas an *international* audience, which in turn allowed the 'art film' to become a marketing device for its country of origin.

The term 'art cinema', when linked to its institutional funding base, actually covers an enormous range of film-making practices – as is evidenced in part by the stylistic diversity of the New German Cinema films, ranging from highly avant-garde work through to more mainstream narratives – but there are some shared broad characteristics. For instance, the films at some level articulate or construct a sense of national identity, and bear markers of their national origin; at a textual level the films often evidence formal characteristics which can be read as signifiers of an authorial voice; historically they have dealt more openly and graphically than Hollywood films with sex and sexuality – so much so that 'art film' became a euphormism for soft porn; and they are usually produced for both international and local consumption (Neale 1981). The term has also been popularly used to refer to a narrower body of films that can be characterised by what David Bordwell has termed their 'art-cinema narration'. This form of narration, when employed, is where the difference between art cinema and Hollywood films is most apparent and is often read as functioning in opposition to the Hollywood narrative form.

According to Bordwell, in such films there can be an objective verisimilitude, with the use of location shooting and non-Hollywood lighting schemes. Linked to this, the tight cause-and-effect narrative structure that characterises Hollywood cinema is replaced by a more tenuous linking of events – there may be calculated gaps in the plot, scenes may be built around chance encounters and a film may be nothing more than a series of them linked together by a trip or a search, events may lead to nothing, resulting in a drifting episodic narrative and a lack of closure. The films also aim to 'exhibit character', but the characters tend to lack clear-cut traits, motives and goals. Protagonists may act inconsistently or question themselves and their purpose. And whereas the Hollywood protagonist speeds towards a goal, the art-film protagonist slides passively from one situation to another. The hero is often a highly sensitive individual who may recount autobiographical events, dreams and the like, or be on the verge of a breakdown. Such films will often display what is termed 'expressive realism' – that is, they dramatise private mental processes which are rarely explained through social forces. So inquiry into character becomes a central concern. The films also tend to deal with the 'human condition' and may pronounce judgments on 'modern life' or deal with current psychological problems such as contemporary 'alienation' and 'lack of communication'. There can also be a marked self-consciousness to aspects of the shooting and editing style which can act as a form of commentary. Thus the films can combine a documentary factuality with an intense psychological subjectivity. And they tend – as Schrader observes above – to invite thought and reflection rather than offer a solution to a problem.

In terms of its institutional funding base and its raison d'être, the New German Cinema clearly forms part of the wider phenomenon of European art cinema. Not all New German Cinema films, however, fit Bordwell's 'art cinema' narrational model, but it is certainly evidenced in a number of them and can provide a productive framework for analysis. Wim Wenders' *Alice in the Cities* (*Alice in den Städten*, 1973), for instance, focuses on Philip Winter, a German journalist trying to write an article in the US. After travelling aimlessly around taking instamatic photos, he fails to produce the article, runs out of money and plans to return to New York. While buying a plane ticket home, Philip meets a young German woman and her daughter Alice who are also returning to Germany. Due to a ground personnel strike in Germany they can only get flights to Amsterdam the following afternoon. They all stay overnight in a hotel, but Alice's mother disappears off in the morning to see to some unfinished business, leaving a note which asks Philip to take Alice on to Amsterdam without her. When she fails to arrive in Amsterdam on the next flight, Philip has the unwanted task of trying to return Alice to her family in Germany. After an unsuccessful day searching Wuppertal for her grandmother, Philip takes Alice to the police, but she runs away and rejoins him. They continue their rather haphazard search for the grandmother, but without success. With nothing better to do, they go swimming and meet up with a young woman who puts them up for the night. The following morning, faced with no money, Philip decides to take Alice to his parents. On the way they are spotted by the police who tell Philip they have found the grandmother and Alice's mother has also turned up. The police put Alice on a train to Munich to be reunited with her mother. Not wanting to part from her new friend, Alice gives Philip some money to buy himself a ticket. The film

FIGURE 3 Alice and Philip search for her mother in *Alice in the Cities* (1973)

ends with them sharing a train compartment and Philip declaring he will finish writing his story in Munich.

Filmed in black and white and shot mostly on location in America, Amsterdam and the Ruhr area of Germany, *Alice in the Cities* can, for instance, be characterised very much in terms of its 'drifting episodic narrative'. The first part of the film follows Philip on a largely fruitless car journey around the US, while the rest of the film hinges purely on the chance encounter with Alice's mother and ends with another chance encounter when Philip and Alice are spotted by the police. A major proportion of the film focuses on Philip in the act of travelling, either alone or accompanied by Alice, with shots of the protagonists in various forms of transport and innumerable tracking shots out of car, coach, airplane, train and monorail windows documenting the attendant landscapes. Thus the film incorporates little conventional dramatic 'action'. Indeed, there are extensive sections in *Alice in the Cities* where effectively nothing 'happens'. When Philip and Alice leave New York, for instance, they are shown in several shots at the airport just waiting for their flight to be called, while a whole seven minutes of film time is used to show them simply passing time during the flight – playing games, going to the toilet, sleeping and so on.

Much of the film is also taken up with exploring Philip's character. Although he appears to have goals – initially that of writing an article and subsequently of returning Alice to her family – he fails in both and is represented as rather directionless. He hands Alice over to the police when the task of finding her grandmother seems impossible, but simply takes off with her when she rejoins him, and is easily persuaded by Alice to continue travelling with her at the end of the film rather than continue on to his parents. He passively accepts what happens to him rather than taking charge of his life.

Also central to the film is Philip's obsession with taking photos and people's reactions to them. When we first see him in the US, he looks at the photos he has taken and says 'They never show what you really see'. Alice also looks at one he takes out of the airplane window and likes it because it's 'so empty', while the policeman who spots them at the end of the film looks at one Philip has just taken before the image has developed and observes 'There's nothing on it'. And in Amsterdam Alice takes a photo of Philip and when she gives it to him we see her face reflected over and blurring the image of his. Thus the film functions as a comment on our image-based and media-saturated society, suggesting the visual media distort or fail to show reality.

It also draws attention to lack of communication as a feature of modern life. Philip's obsession with images, for instance, and their relation to the reality he sees around him has rendered him incapable of writing his article and hence communicating with other people. Language barriers also present problems. Alice's mother cannot communicate with the airline personnel in New York because her English is poor, while in Amsterdam Alice – who has lived there and speaks Dutch – has to translate a restaurant menu for Philip. But even sharing the same language is no guarantee of being able to communicate. Time and again, when Philip enters into conversations with other Germans, they fail to listen to each other properly, or ignore each other's questions and talk about their own concerns instead.

Thus, the film clearly fits Bordwell's 'art cinema' narrational model and can easily be read as working in opposition to the Hollywood narrative form. In so far as many 'art films' from other European countries also fit Bordwell's model, *Alice in the Cities* can in fact be viewed as a typically European film as well as a specifically German one. Indeed, Philip's unceasing travelling (through different countries) seems indicative of the rootlessness thought to in part characterise the contemporary experience of being 'European'. And by reading *Alice in the Cities* within this framework, the film becomes more of a general exploration of character and the modern condition – especially in connection with the role of the mass media in society – which has a relevance that extends beyond national boundaries.

Yet, the focus on Philip and Alice as Germans trying to return to their homeland, together with the location filming in the country's Ruhr region, obviously draws attention to the film's national origins. It is undeniably a *German* film, and this is reinforced by the way it can also be understood as a product of *Sensibilismus*, a specifically German tendency or attitude that privileged direct and subjective experience of the world. 'Sensibilism', as it is translated, flourished in Munich during the late 1960s and influenced students – Wenders among them – at the city's film and television school, the HFF. Although Wenders graduated from the HFF three years before making *Alice in the Cities*, the film fits Eric Rentschler's description of the films made by Munich's Sensibilists almost exactly:

> [They] made films with extended travelling shots and long takes. They pointed their cameras out of apartment and car windows onto the streets. The works had a contemplative tenor and very little if any story line; they consisted of series of images meant to capture the ineffable feel of things. (1984: 174)

In balancing its specifically German references, origins and influences with more general and universal themes, *Alice in the Cities* is a good example of how art cinema films can operate for both local and international consumption. However, for the New German Cinema films, reaching the domestic market entailed addressing a number of problems in relation to questions of distribution and exhibition.

Distribution and exhibition

As with other national art cinemas, the New German Cinema generated its own distribution and exhibition networks which were essential to its survival. Although many of the films made an impact on the international art cinema and film festival circuits, by the early 1970s there was not a single commercial distributor in West Germany that was not US-controlled, and consequently the new directors had no guarantee that their films would get taken into distribution and hence exhibited in cinemas to domestic audiences. According to Rentschler, 'in April 1970 it was reported that nineteen Young German films could not find a distributor' (1984: 46). And Elsaesser has reported that by the following year 'over 30 full-length feature films produced with public money had failed to find any form of exhibition other than occasional screenings at festivals or in the presence of the director' (1989: 26). Thus, it became apparent very early on that if 'a renewal of the German film' was to take place, it was not enough simply to fund production work. As the film subsidy system developed therefore increasing attention was paid to the distribution and exhibition sectors, with the BMI, the FFA and the Kuratorium all channelling some of their funding into these areas from 1970 onwards. For example, in April 1970 the BMI started offering subsidies to cinemas which had screened a so-called 'suitable quota' of 'good' German films; and from December 1976 it introduced awards for distributors who had released quality-rated or state-subsidised German films.

Kuratorium funding enabled a small production company called *Basis Film* to take on the distribution of their first film, *Dear Mother, I'm OK (Liebe Mutter, mir geht es gut*, 1971), when no existing distributor showed any interest in releasing it. Directed by Christian Ziewer, it was one of the first in the series of *Arbeiterfilme* produced by the Cologne television station WDR in the late 1960s and early 1970s. *Dear Mother* is about a mechanic who through losing his job gradually comes to understand the social and

39

political conditions that prevent workers like himself from improving their situation. Filmed in a very detached, static and analytical style, the film proved too demanding for commercial distributors and cinemas. Their experience with this film made Basis recognise the need for a company that specialised in distributing the less commercially orientated, more socially critical films that many of the new young directors were making. They set up their own distribution wing, *Basis-Film Verleih* and, in addition to their own productions, distributed films by Helga Reidemeister, Cristina Perinciola, Helma Sanders-Brahms, Peter Lilienthal, Helke Sander, Rosa von Praunheim, Ulrike Ottinger, Harun Farocki, Marianne Rosenbaum and others. In order to help build up audiences for such films – often among trade union organisations, political associations, factory workers, church groups, women's projects, youth groups, film clubs and educational institutions – they supplied background material to accompany the films and inform post-screening discussions, as well as arranging for directors to attend screenings.

In 1971 a group of 13 film-makers – among them Wenders, Fassbinder, Hans W. Geissendörfer and Thomas Schamoni – took their own initiative and founded the loosely structured collective *Filmverlag der Autoren* (Film Publishing House of the Auteurs). Filmverlag was also originally set up as a production company, but it quickly moved into and prioritised distribution. However, in contrast to Basis, Filmverlag identified a need to actively promote the new German films to national and international cinema audiences, and under the management initially of Laurens Straub and then Mathias Ginsberg implemented American-style marketing campaigns. Their success was such that Filmverlag became more or less competitive with the large American distributors and in 1977 restructured from its small cooperative status to give a 55 per cent controlling interest to the publisher Rudolf Augstein, while the founding film-makers became minority shareholders.

Despite such initiatives and their relative successes, cinema audiences for New German Cinema films on their home market remained small – indeed, by the late 1970s the *total* output of German films (commercial and art cinema releases combined) had less than a 10 per cent share of the home market. Writing in 1980 Volker Schlöndorff commented that largely due to the anti-establishment politics of some their films, the Filmverlag 'doesn't touch more than 400 cinemas out of 3,800 which is absolutely minimal; and most of the others refuse purely and simply to do business with the Filmverlag' (in Corrigan 1994: 57). The perception that New German Cinema films were unpopular with domestic audiences was further fuelled by the fact that – as discussed earlier – few of them were box-office successes, a fact that elicited some criticism at home. In 1977, for instance, Eckart Schmidt declared: 'Film-makers like Kluge, Herzog, Geissendörfer and Fassbinder, all of whom have collected subsidies more than once, and who despite such public funding are incapable of directing a success, should in future be barred from receiving subsidies. Film subsidy is no pension fund for failed film-makers' (in Elsaesser 1989: 37).

However, within the existing exhibition system, it was virtually impossible for a German film to reach a mass audience – and hence return a profit – unless it was released through an American distributor. As Elsaesser explains:

> If a production took more than DM500,000 to make, it could not return its investment on the second-run or art cinema circuits. Yet, unless it cost more than 5 million, the Majors were rarely interested, since for an American distributor the economics of starting films in first-run cinemas are such that only above a certain budget (equated with certain production values) does it become viable to invest in sufficient prints, pre-publicity and local advertising to properly launch a new release. (1989: 38)

The New German Cinema films, dependent upon modest public subsidy and television finance, were usually caught between these two sets of figures and effectively in a no-win situation – although in later years some of the more successful directors were distributed by the US majors. In addition, their very diversity – part of their distinctiveness and strength – also made them difficult to classify generically and hence equally difficult to market to a potential audience within the parameters of commercial cinema. With the growth of television viewing as a leisure pursuit, together with the demise of the traditional family audience and the rise of the student protest movement in the late 1960s, cinema audiences had also become highly fragmented. In West Germany as in other countries viewers were becoming younger, and cinema was looked to for both blockbuster spectacles and cult films, as well as for information and education. This combination of factors, together with the absence of a developed film culture in Germany (outside 'centres' like Berlin, Hamburg and Munich), meant that the odds were stacked against the New German Cinema finding a national audience.

However, to counter the hostility of their critics at home – and for the sake of their own professional self-esteem – the new directors were keen to try and find audiences for their work. Hence the promotion of an *Autorenkino* – with its privileging of the notion of film as a means of personal expression – gave way to a greater concern with making films that related to the experiences of viewers, that dealt with matters of social relevance, and offered interesting and credible identificatory figures. This is unsurprising in some ways, since the student protest movement that swept across Europe in the late 1960s and early 1970s and its concern with the Vietnam war had politicised a whole generation and raised their critical awareness of the media. As television was slow to respond to the information needs of this generation, they looked to cinema as one possible alternative source of political information. If the new directors were to attract this sizeable audience, they had to adapt – even if only in the wider sense – to their political needs. Elsaesser suggests that it is this shift to addressing a clearly identified spectator that in part differentiates the New German Cinema from the Young German Film (1989: 154). And it also distinguishes it from other art cinemas, which were less concerned with social issues and less aware of a political role for film.

Although young people were in fact starting to return to the cinema, looking especially for something different to the experience offered by television, the search for film audiences mostly happened outside of the commercial cinema circuit. Television in fact offered access to significant pre-existing audiences – especially to those groups such as women, gays and other 'minorities' whose concerns have been largely excluded by commercial cinema – and proved to be an important form of exhibition for a number of women film-makers. The remit of a small workshop department at ZDF called *Das kleine Fernsehspiel*, for instance, was to develop new forms of television and promote aesthetic experiment. In pursuit of these aims they commissioned a far higher proportion of women directors than was normal. Although its late-night programming slot could still severely limit the number of viewers for a film, during the late 1970s the films made by women consistently achieved well above average viewing figures when broadcast. Indeed, television precisely allowed film-makers to target their work at more clearly defined audiences, and Elsaesser reports: 'In most cases audiences responded very much in direct proportion to recognising themselves and their own problems on screen' (1989: 152).

Some film-makers – including Kluge, Herzog and Werner Schroeter, among others – attended screenings of their work at film clubs and film festivals and participated in discussions with the audiences in order to try and attract a new audience for their films. However, a key factor in developing domestic audiences for the New German Cinema was the setting up of *Kommunale Kinos* across the country. Initiated by the Frankfurt Senator of Cultural Affairs in the early 1970s, these were art house or programme cinemas funded by local authority grants. Largely relieved of commercial pressures and practices, they greatly increased the exhibition outlets for new German films and, perhaps more importantly, helped foster the development of a film culture that brought more people into contact with the cinema.

The New German Cinema directors had an easier time attracting audiences abroad – partly because outside of Germany, the films were to an extent divorced from their concrete socio-political context, which allowed them to be more readily marketed as 'art cinema' to established audiences. The films of Hans-Jürgen Syberberg, for instance, have always had a rough ride with German audiences and critics alike, while they have proved more popular in the US. As Syberberg has asserted with regard to his film *Hitler, A Film From Germany* (*Hitler – Ein Film aus Deutschland*, 1976–77): 'In Frankfurt, during the six days of its showing, one hundred and fifty people in all saw *Hitler*. In San Francisco in three days alone more people saw it than all those who saw it in Frankfurt, Munich, and Hamburg combined' (in Corrigan 1994: 203). Such success abroad can rekindle interest on the home front, as was the case with Herzog's *The Enigma of*

Kaspar Hauser (Jeder für sich und Gott gegen alle, 1974). After a luke-warm reception on its initial release in Germany, *Kaspar Hauser* did very well in the US and at European festivals, and as a consequence then achieved greater success back in Germany. But this has tended to be the exception rather than the rule for New German Cinema films.

Thus, over the years, the New German Cinema gradually built up a range of fairly diverse audiences for its films. The recognition of the importance of such audiences in sustaining a film culture, however, represents a significant shift from the position declared in the Oberhausen Manifesto. And that shift was brought about partly through the new cinema's increasing reliance on television funding and television's need to target its pre-existing audiences. This change of position on the part of the film-makers was publicly acknowledged in another manifesto, the so-called Hamburg Declaration, made in 1979. In 1962 the focus – necessarily in some ways – was on the film-makers alone, their needs and their rights, irrespective of what the German public might actually want. By the end of the 1970s, having to some extent established themselves and learned by the experience, their stance had been tempered:

> On the occasion of the Hamburg Film Festival we German film-makers have come together. Seventeen years after Oberhausen we have taken stock. ... We have proved our professionalism. That does not mean we have to see ourselves as a guild. We have learned that our only allies can be the spectators. That means the people who work, who have wishes, dreams, and desires, that means the people who go to the movies and who do not, and that also means people who can imagine a totally different kind of film.

And it is possible to argue that this shift in position played a key role in enabling the New German Cinema to make a significant contribution to international film culture.

2   ACHIEVEMENTS: COUNTER-MYTHS OF GERMAN IDENTITY

Dealing with contemporary reality

The New German Cinema may have experienced difficulties in finding a national cinema audience and its directors for the most part remained marginal figures in the industry, but by the end of the 1970s it had clearly established itself and made its mark, especially on the international cinema scene. The films had won innumerable festival prizes – both at home and abroad – and were programmed regularly as special seasons at arts cinemas and Goethe Institutes in cities such as New York and London, while a number of their directors were internationally acclaimed. A steady flow of literature on West Germany's new cinema also began to be published, with various books and special issues of film journals appearing, especially in the US and Britain. Why did the films make such an impression and generate such interest? Even at home, a number of them did achieve relatively high viewing figures – with even a handful of commercial successes – and win critical acclaim. What made them so significant?

It is possible to argue that a number of factors were involved, such as the extraordinary talents of the directors, the attempt to create a new film language, and the challenging aim of developing a cinema that was both culturally motivated and economically viable. However, a key element was the fact that most of the films engaged with contemporary concerns in a way that contrasted sharply with the largely 'escapist' nature of 1950s German cinema – especially its reluctance to address recent history. For instance, a classic *Heimatfilm* from the mid-1950s, Harald Reinl's *The Fisherwoman from Lake Constance* (*Die Fischerin vom Bodensee*, 1956), shows people living in harmony with their surroundings with no evidence of war damage or post-war reconstruction. For the new generation of film-makers who were all born around the time of the Second World War and grew up in a post-war divided Germany, such films were a blatant denial of the realities of contemporary German life. If there was to be a renewal of German cinema, then its films had necessarily to tackle contemporary issues in some way. For instance, *It* (*Es*, 1965) by Ulrich Schamoni addressed the question of abortion at a time when it was still illegal in Germany, while Schlöndorff's *Young Törless* (*Der junge Törless*, 1966) used the story – adapted from a Robert Musil novel originally published in 1906 – of a young boy's experience of two fellow pupils at a boarding school torturing a Jewish boy to raise questions about the Nazi past.

Thus, the majority of New German Cinema films demonstrated a contemporary relevance virtually unprecedented in the history of West German cinema. Indeed, they can be characterised as an endeavour to represent a contemporary reality that had previously been largely excluded from post-war German cinema, or as Eric Rentschler has aptly expressed it, as 'the quest for alternative images and counter-representations' (1984: 4). What follows here is a discussion of a number of the contemporary concerns that recur across the new cinema's films – namely the presence of the *Gastarbeiter*, the rise of urban terrorism in the 1970s, the Nazi past, the experience of American cultural imperialism, and the influence of the women's movement – together with textual analyses of a range of films, in order to explore some of those counter-representations.

The Gastarbeiter, exploitation and prejudice

When the Federal Republic started to enjoy economic prosperity in the 1950s it gradually moved towards virtually full employment, despite the fact that 3 million East Germans had taken refuge there since its creation in 1949. As production continued to increase and once the erection of the

Berlin Wall in 1961 prevented further migration from the East, it became necessary to import foreign labour in order to sustain West German industries. By 1969 over 1.5 million Turks, Italians and Greeks were employed there, with the Turks constituting a sizeable majority. These so-called *Gastarbeiter* (guest workers) were regarded by successive German governments as temporary labour and could in theory be sent home if unemployment amongst Germans ever became acute. However, due to the lack of a comprehensively formulated policy, the workers proved in practice to be anything but transitory. Many *Gastarbeiter* remained in the Federal Republic year after year, often establishing their families and raising their children there. Although some did return home to their own countries, West Germany's *Gastarbeiter* became a more or less permanent element of the country's population, something which by the 1980s was reflected in a favouring of the term *Fremdarbeiter* (foreign workers) over the increasingly inappropriate *Gastartbeiter*.

When West Germany's 'economic miracle' began to wane in the early 1970s, however, this meant the country was faced with a growing, semi-permanent non-German population who needed education, housing and other resources, but were themselves no longer needed by their host society and thus became increasingly prone to racist attack. By the early 1980s anti-Turkish racism in particular was widespread, especially amongst the younger generation, which in turn had elicited warnings from the older generation against allowing a modern day equivalent of the Nazis' anti-semitism to develop.

Both Fassbinder and Helma Sanders-Brahms have addressed the presence of the *Gastarbeiter* in West Germany in a number of their films: Fassbinder in *Katzelmacher* (1969), *Wild Game* (*Wildwechsel*, 1972) and *Fear Eats the Soul* (*Angst essen Seele auf*, 1973), and Sanders-Brahms in *The Industrial Reserve Army* (*Die industrielle Reservearmee*, 1971) and *Shirin's Wedding* (*Shirins Hochzeit*, 1975). These films tackle the *Gastarbeiter* issue in different ways, but they all draw attention to their presence in the Federal Republic and contextualise their specific situation within wider issues.

Made in black and white, *Shirin's Wedding*, for instance, is the moving story of Shirin, a young Turkish woman who goes in search of

Mahmud, the man she was betrothed to as a child. Mahmud is a guest worker in Germany and on his last visit home to their village appeared to have forgotten all about Shirin. Faced with another arranged marriage, Shirin flees to Istanbul and leaves for Germany. Set in the 1970s, the film shows her making a promising start in the Federal Republic working at a factory and living in a women's hostel, regularly sending money home and looking for Mahmud in her spare time. When she is made redundant, she moves in with a Greek family who have befriended her and takes an office cleaning job. But when she is raped by one of the company's employees and the Greek family return home, Shirin is faced with no job and nowhere to live. She is picked up by a pimp, Aida, who teams her up with two other prostitutes to work the men's hostels at night. In one of these hostels she finally encounters Mahmud, who barely recognises her and pays for her services like all the other guest workers. One night Shirin decides to return to Turkey and tries to run off, but one of the pimps shoots and kills her.

While her decision to go to West Germany is motivated by personal circumstances, the film locates Shirin's personal story within the wider context of the guest worker situation generally. When Shirin applies for work at the German Labour Office in Istanbul, for instance, we see shots of the waiting room, of Shirin being weighed, having a medical examination, giving blood, signing papers, and of her subsequently waiting at the airport with hundreds of others for her flight to Germany. At the same time a voice-over commentary says how long the process takes, explains how all those travelling from Turkey to Germany are leaving behind their families, homes and villages, and how hundreds of fellow Turks wait to leave 'not just with you, but every night'. This documentary or observational aspect is reinforced through extensive use of medium to long shots, with relatively few close-ups, and a fairly static camera throughout the film.

Although the film does address the situation of the guest workers in this way, through the figure of Shirin it also explores and acts as an observation on what happens when two very different cultures meet. There are the inevitable misunderstandings, both humorous and otherwise. Shirin, for instance, declares in voice-over that she never understood German beds and is scolded by a hostel attendant for making hers up incorrectly, while in the factory a flirtatious manager upsets Shirin by pulling her headscarf off because he does not realise she believes she will go to hell if a man sees her hair. There are, however, more serious consequences. When Shirin is raped, according to her culture's value system the loss of her virginity means she can no longer marry. In a few minutes her whole purpose in life has been destroyed – she can no longer marry Mahmud. The brutal nature of this meeting between Turkish and German culture is reinforced and elucidated through a conversational voice-over that runs through much of the film between Shirin and a sympathetic German female voice. They discuss Shirin's experiences and when it comes to her experience of being made redundant, the German female voice comments: 'My country brought you in like cattle, housed you like cattle, grew fat on your labour, and discarded you when no longer needed. Cattle are treated better.'

Hence the encounter between the Turkish and German cultures is represented as being very destructive of the former, with the blame laid squarely at the feet of the latter. Although the film appears at one level to be about the plight of the (female) guest worker, it is also addressing the Federal Republic's treatment of those workers. This is evident in the way that Shirin is represented very much as a victim and her 'descent' into the seedy world of prostitution, together with her death, as virtually inevitable. She is unable to survive in a European culture and comes to signify Germany's ruthlessness as a colonising power. While *Shirin's Wedding* certainly exposes the unpleasant underbelly of West Germany's economic miracle, it is possible to argue that the film is more about the country's 'guilt' with regard to its treatment of the guest workers, than about Shirin – even though she is the central protagonist – and the lived experiences of the guest workers. This may in turn account for the extremely negative response the film elicited from the Turkish community (including death threats for the actress who played Shirin) when it was broadcast on German television in 1976.

Fassbinder's films are similarly less concerned with exploring the experiences of the *Gastarbeiter* themselves, than with exploring and critiquing some of the attitudes towards them. *Katzelmacher* – a Bavarian term of abuse for immigrant workers – for instance, revolves around a group of directionless young couples who live in a suburban block of flats. With little to interest or motivate them, the arrival of a Greek *Gastarbeiter*,

Jorgos (played by Fassbinder himself), unleashes what critics saw at the time as the fascist tendencies that were still latent in West German society. As the women gradually become curious about Jorgos it arouses the jealousies of their respective male partners. The situation starts to become antagonistic, with the men getting increasingly violent towards 'their' women and eventually beating up Jorgos. A very stylised film, *Katzelmacher* thereby suggests that any perception that the *Gastarbeiter* were unwelcome in West Germany had as much, if not more, to do with attitudes that already existed within German society as with the situation that developed after their arrival.

This exploration of latent prejudices is examined and developed further in Fassbinder's later film, *Fear Eats the Soul*. Starting with the subtitle 'Happiness is not always fun', the film follows the growing relationship between Emmi, a short dumpy middle-aged widow with three married children, and Ali, a tall handsome Moroccan *Gastarbeiter* some twenty years her junior. They meet when Emmi shelters from the rain in a bar frequented by Ali and his fellow guest workers. The two hit it off, Ali escorts Emmi home and spends the night with her. Unexpectedly they fall in love and marry, but are unprepared for the latent prejudice against guest workers that surfaces among Emmi's children, her neighbours, and the women with whom she works. Initially very happy together, other people's attitudes gradually get Emmi down as she is increasingly ostracised for marrying a foreigner. When she and Ali return from a holiday, however, Emmi finds her family and friends more accepting of her marriage because they need her help in some way. As she is reintegrated into her old social circle, she becomes less considerate towards Ali, who in turn seeks out his old guest worker friends and starts sleeping with the young woman who owns the bar where he and Emmi met. As their relationship starts to fall apart, Emmi becomes distraught and Ali begins gambling. In an attempt to salvage something, Emmi returns to the bar where once again they fall into conversation and reaffirm their love for one another. However, Ali collapses, is rushed to hospital and diagnosed with a perforated stomach ulcer – something the doctor tells Emmi is common among guest workers. The prognosis is not good, but Emmi remains hopeful about their future together.

FIGURE 4 Emmi and Ali reaffirm their love in *Fear Eats the Soul* (1973)

As with *Shirin's Wedding*, the film highlights cultural differences between the guest workers and their host society, but the main focus is on the extremely racist attitudes towards the guest workers. Emmi's son-in-law Eugen refers to them as 'swine' and cannot accept the fact that he has to report to a Turkish foreman at work, while her daughter Krista refuses to stay in 'this pigsty' when Emmi invites her children round to her flat to meet Ali. Other characters make reference to guest workers like Ali being 'dirty' and 'filthy'. Emmi's neighbours insist that she take additional turns cleaning the communal stairs in her block of flats since 'when one of them lives in a place it always gets filthy', while later, on meeting Ali, her workmates express genuine surprise at his cleanliness.

Emmi, in her turn, becomes 'contaminated' by association. She is, for instance, repeatedly referred to as a whore for having a relationship with Ali. On meeting Ali, her son Albert declares: 'You can forget you ever had children. I want nothing to do with a whore.' Initially, her workmates simply refuse to talk to her, while her local grocer refuses to serve her and throws her out of his shop. Indeed, one of her neighbours explains Emmi's willingness to consort with a foreigner by the fact that with a surname like Kurowski (her first husband having been Polish), Emmi herself cannot be 'a real German'.

Fassbinder reinforces how these prejudices isolate the characters by repeatedly framing them in doorways. When Ali and Emmi first meet and marry, they are often filmed through a doorway, sitting together. Their happiness and pleasure in each other's company means they are not alone, but it underlines the fact that their relationship sets them apart. Later, as their relationship starts to deteriorate, they are both framed separately, filmed again through doorways, standing alone. As the strain of living with racism takes its toll, they are isolated not only from their social circle but from each other.

However, the fact that Emmi and Ali marry also makes their relationship one that has to be publicly acknowledged, it cannot be politely ignored. This draws attention to the age difference – and Emmi's age in particular – and it is possible to argue that the reaction to the couple's relationship stems as much from this as it does from racist attitudes. At the beginning of the film, for instance, an attractive young German woman in the bar makes advances towards Ali, which he rejects. When he later invites her and his guest worker friends back to Emmi's flat, she refuses to go to that 'old whore's'. This implies that it is acceptable for her to have a sexual relationship with Ali, but not for someone like Emmi. Furthermore, other characters refer to the marriage as 'disgraceful' and 'indecent', hinting at a perceived impropriety for a woman of Emmi's age to have a loving sexual relationship. The relationship also arouses incredulity. For instance, when Emmi first tells her daughter Krista that she has fallen in love with Ali, twenty years her junior, she and her husband Eugen burst out laughing. And when their relationship is falling apart, Emmi visits Ali at his workplace, where – despite her emotional pleas – his colleagues cannot acknowledge the true nature of their relationship, preferring instead to joke about her being his grandmother from Morocco.

This added dimension brings a greater complexity to the *Gastarbeiter* theme, suggesting that prejudices are not clear cut. It also introduces a more universal theme of intolerance – something which is very much at odds with the ideals embodied in the constitution of the Federal Republic, but which also gives the film wider relevance. Indeed, Emmi interprets the attitudes they encounter as emanating from basic human jealousy of their happiness, as implied in the film's subtitle. Although the film's narrative resolution suggests their problems in all their complexity will not simply go away (and several characters predict the relationship will not last), these wider issues may help account for the film's international success. Not only did it win the International Critics Prize at Cannes in 1974, but it attracted a much wider audience with cinema and television screenings in many countries.

Films were subsequently made in West Germany which did explore the experiences of the guest workers from their own perspective – and tried to raise awareness of those experiences – such as Tevfik Baser's *40 Square Metres of Germany* (*40m² Deutschland*, 1986) and Günter Wallraff's *The Lowest of the Low* (*Ganz Unten*, 1985–86). Based on his own experience, Baser's film, for instance, conveyed a sense of the isolation many Turkish immigrants have asserted they felt when they first went to the Federal Republic which contrasts dramatically to the camaraderie and friendship Shirin enjoys at the hostel where she lives and the factory where she works, while in *The Lowest of the Low* renowned writer and journalist Wallraff went undercover to expose the appalling work conditions of immigrant workers at the industrial plants in the heart of the Ruhr area. And other films – such as Jo Schäfer's *Cemil* (1985) and *On the Edge of Dreams* (*Am Rande der Träume*, 1985) made by West Berlin's *Medienoperative*, an independent video group who had been working with the local Turkish community since 1979 – started to address the experiences of Turkish *Gastarbeiter* children who had been born, or at least educated, in Germany and identified more closely with the European culture of their German contemporaries than with the Turkish culture of their parents.

In contrast, it is possible to argue that both *Shirin's Wedding* and *Fear Eats the Soul* are primarily concerned with exploring what happens when two different cultures meet, something which has of course increasingly become part of the European experience generally. While they address the resulting exploitation of and racism towards those colonised, the films are more centrally concerned with the attitudes of the colonising nation than with the workers' experiences. Consequently, the films act as a powerful reminder of the Nazis' anti-semitism, implying such attitudes continue to exist in the Federal Republic, and undermine the country's image as a new political democracy.

The violence of politics

During the 1970s a number of film-makers also turned their attention to the increasing terrorist activity that was disrupting German life and stemmed largely from political developments during the 1960s. Although West Germany's right-wing Christian Democratic Union (CDU) had enjoyed undisputed power under the leadership of Konrad Adenauer during the 1950s, in 1962 a political scandal seriously undermined their power. A left-wing journalist published secret details of NATO manoeuvres and in retaliation the CDU's Minister for Defence had the journalist concerned arrested, while police occupied the offices of his employer. These actions caused both a national and international outcry, and the Minister had to resign. At the next elections in 1966 the CDU failed to achieve an outright majority, forcing them to form a coalition government – the so-called Great Coalition – with the Social Democratic Party of Germany (SPD).

The SPD was the only legal party on the left in West Germany after the German Communist Party was outlawed in 1956. At the end of the 1950s, however, it had distanced itself from its Marxist origins which undermined its position as an alternative to the conservative status quo and rendered support for it by left-wing intellectuals problematic. When they formed the Great Coalition with the CDU, with Kurt Georg Kiesinger, a former Nazi, as Chancellor, it meant that there was effectively no longer any parliamentary opposition on the left. This situation led to the growth of an extra-parliamentary opposition movement, known as APO (*Außerparlamentarische Opposition*), which found its most ardent supporters among left-wing students campaigning for reform of the University system and disappointed at how little social change had been effected since the end of the war. They were, for instance, extremely critical precisely of the fact that ex-Nazis such as Kiesinger had been able to attain prominent and powerful positions in the new Federal Republic, and their numbers swelled the APO ranks considerably. As large numbers of students took to the streets in protest, the government drew up a series of laws that would provide for a possible state of emergency – the so-called *Notstandgesetze*. For the left-wing APO, this had alarming echoes of similar emergency measures taken by the Nazis in the 1930s to outlaw the Left and suspend parliament.

These political developments at home galvinised what had been a growing student protest movement, but international politics provided the movement with additional impetus. Opposition to US foreign policy, especially with regard to America's involvement in Vietnam, fuelled student protest in the late 1960s not only in Germany but across Europe and in America itself. In Germany it led to a student protest against a visit to Berlin in 1967 by the then Shah of Iran, who was seen as a US puppet and violator of human rights. In a mass demonstration, the students were attacked by the police which resulted in the death of one student, Benno Ohnesorg, who was shot in the back. Although it had tragic consequences, the police response to the student protest suggested the movement was perceived as a real and powerful threat, and this in turn mobilised even greater numbers of students. The outcry against the police actions were such that 10,000 people attended Ohnesorg's funeral and there were demonstrations all over West Germany.

Protest actions continued, especially against the Springer press which had vilified the students from the outset in its popular national daily newspaper, the tabloid *Bild*, and for a while the student movement seemed unstoppable. But it underestimated the power and resilience of the state, its institutions, and especially the media. It was unable to bring down the Springer press, and also failed to prevent the passing of the *Notstandgesetze* into law – with the support of the SPD – in 1968. Moreover, towards the end of the 1960s the political situation changed. In 1968 the German Communist Party was allowed to reform, increasing the possibility of parliamentary opposition on the left. And the following year the Great Coalition collapsed, bringing the SPD to power in their own right and making Willy Brandt the next Chancellor. Although the party's past record did not offer left-wing intellectuals much hope for the future, Brandt's impeccable record of opposition to Nazism did make his government a more acceptable alternative to the Great Coalition under the leadership of Kiesinger. Thus, as the 1960s came to a close, the student protest movement in Germany – already fragmenting due to internal political differences – started to collapse, and optimistic hopes largely gave way to a sense of powerlessness and open resignation.

However, a small number of left-wing extremists refused to give up the fight for socio-political change and turned to violence. Sporadic terrorist acts such as bombings, bank robberies and arson attacks had in fact started as early as 1968. A couple of years later terrorist Andreas Baader met the journalist Ulrike Meinhof, and together they set up the Baader-Meinhof terrorist group which later became the Red Army Faction (RAF). Although Baader and Meinhof were both arrested in 1972 – together with fellow terrorist Gudrun Ensslin – other RAF members escalated terrorist actions throughout the 1970s. The government took increasingly repressive measures, but largely without success, and events came to a head in autumn 1977. In the September the RAF kidnapped the prominent industrialist and former Nazi Hanns-Martin Schleyer and demanded the release of eleven terrorists for his safe return, but the government refused. The following month the RAF hijacked a Lufthansa plane, taking it to Mogadishu in Somalia, with fatal consequences for the hijackers when anti-terrorist troops stormed the plane. The next day Baader, Ensslin and a third imprisoned terrorist, Carl Raspe, were found dead in their prison cells. The official version of their deaths was suicide, but they had been held in Stammheim, a new high-security prison, and some cast doubt on the possibility of them gaining access to the means to take their own lives – implying that the imprisoned terrorists had in fact been murdered. As if in retaliation, Schleyer was found dead a few days later.

Several films were made which directly or indirectly addressed the issues raised by this terrorist activity and the state's response to it. One director who has returned to the theme repeatedly is Margarethe von Trotta. Her first solo feature, for instance, *The Second Awakening of Christa Klages* (*Das zweite Erwachen der Christa Klages*, 1977), is based on the true-life story of a woman who robbed a bank to try and keep open a child-care centre threatened with closure, while her later film *The German*

Sisters (*Die bleierne Zeit*, 1981) was made after she met Christiane Ensslin, the sister of dead terrorist Gudrun Ensslin, and explores the relationship between the two sisters. However, it is her first film, *The Lost Honour of Katharina Blum* (*Die verlorene Ehre der Katharina Blum*, 1975), co-directed with Volker Schlöndorff, that explores most directly some of the issues arising from the terrorist activity in West Germany during the mid-1970s.

Based on a Heinrich Böll novel of the same name published in 1974, *The Lost Honour of Katharina Blum* explores how a young woman's life is destroyed at the hands of the police and the press after she unwittingly becomes involved with a man wanted by the police. Böll wrote the novel after he was attacked by the Springer tabloid *Bild* for an article he wrote for the left-wing news magazine *Der Spiegel*. Calling for a stop to the way in which Ulrike Meinhof was effectively being tried by the press after her arrest in 1972, Böll was branded a terrorist sympathiser.

A fairly close adaptation of the book, the film shows how Katharina, a respectable and modest young woman, known as 'the nun' due to her unimpeachable character, meets Ludwig at a carnival party. The two have never met before but are drawn to each other, and uncharacteristically Katharina takes him home and they spend the night together. Ludwig confides to Katharina that he is on the run from the police and she helps him leave her apartment building undetected by the police who have him under surveillance. The following morning the police burst into the apartment, but on finding Ludwig already gone, take Katharina in for questioning. An unscrupulous reporter called Tötges from the *Zeitung* paper exploits his police contacts and seeks out Katharina's relations and acquaintances – even pestering her mother on her hospital deathbed – in search of a good story. Tötges embellishes the facts to make sensationalist copy, suggesting that Katharina's flat may have been 'the seat of a conspiracy, a mob-hideout, a weapon cache', and she makes front page news for several days, leaving her reputation ruined. After a combination of police interrogation, press harassment, hate mail and obscene phone calls, Katharina phones Ludwig from her aunt's, unaware the phone is tapped. After the police capture him, she agrees to grant Tötges an interview and meets him at her flat, where she shoots him. When she is arrested, she sees Ludwig briefly and they embrace before the police escort them to their respective cells. The film ends with an epilogue depicting Tötges' funeral which is attended by local dignitaries and celebrates his bravery.

As is evident, the film is not about the actual terrorist activity that was plaguing West Germany at the time. Towards the end of the film Ludwig is in fact revealed to be only an army deserter who has absconded with army funds – he has not even robbed a bank, as one character observes. Rather, it appears – especially given Böll's reasons for writing the novel on which it is based – to be about what can happen to an innocent, law-abiding individual when misrepresented by the press. That is, sensationalist reporting can influence how the individual concerned is treated which can in turn have unwarrented consequences. For a German audience the similarities between the fictional *Zeitung* and the real-life *Bild* are obvious, and the film can easily be read as a critique of *Bild*'s practices. Indeed, the film ends with the following disclaimer: 'Characters and events are fictitious. Should the description of certain journalistic practices bear any similarity to the practices of the *Bild-Zeitung*, this is neither intentional, nor fortuitous, but unavoidable.' Thus, at one level Ludwig and his 'wanted by the police' status is merely a narrative device to trigger the media defamation of Katharina's character.

However, the police response to Ludwig's crime suggests he is perceived as a major threat to society – and it far outweighs the actual danger he presents. Teams of armed police surround Katharina's building after she has taken him back there, and perform a dramatic 'dawn raid' on her apartment the following morning, forcing the front door open and issuing warnings over a megaphone. Similarly, when Ludwig is caught, his country hideout is surrounded by hundreds of police, dozens of vans, armoured vehicles, and helicopters. Again, the parallels between fiction and the reality of living in a society dogged by urban terrorism are inescapable. Indeed, in the course of the film, a number of statements and references are made which directly suggest or imply Ludwig is a terrorist. For instance, after the dawn raid on Katharina's apartment, the District Attorney tells the press it is clear that they are dealing with 'one or several terrorists, militarily organised with little regard for human life'. Any left-wing connections among Katharina's relations and acquaintances are also played up by the press. The mother of Katharina's aunt, for instance, lives voluntarily in East Germany, while the father has emigrated to the Soviet Union. And Katharina's single act of violence is viewed by the state and its representatives as an assault on democratic values: in an eulogy given at Tötges' funeral, the speaker declares that everyone feels 'the breath of terror, the savagery of anarchy, the violence which is undermining the foundations of our liberal-democratic order, which is so dear to us'.

Hence the film, made in 1975, also works as a critique of the indirect effects of terrorism on West German society, suggesting that anyone can come under suspicion, even for simply behaving out of character. In such a political climate, the state's response to a perceived threat becomes characterised by a heavy-handed over-reaction which can in turn have serious consequences not only for those directly posing the threat, but for anyone who can for any reason – however remote – be tarred by the same brush. Interestingly, *The Lost Honour of Katharina Blum* was – along with Herzog's *The Enigma of Kaspar Hauser* (1974), Fassbinder's *The Marriage of Maria Braun* (1978) and Schlöndorff's *The Tin Drum* (1979) – one of the few New German Cinema films to be commercially successful in German cinemas.

However, it was perhaps the combined incidents of autumn 1977 two years later and the two public funerals they resulted in that had the most profound effect on West German society, prompting questions about Germany and its past among both the younger and older generations. On the one hand, Hanns-Martin Schleyer, a member of the SS under Nazism, was given the honour of a full state funeral in Stuttgart, while the death of the terrorists in Stammheim, a suburb of Stuttgart, generated a controversy about whether their families should be allowed to bury them properly. Local opinion was fiercely opposed to their burial within the city, but the mayor – Manfred Rommel, son of Field Marshall Rommel who was forced to commit suicide by Hitler in 1944 and then given a state funeral – insisted on the families' right to organise a funeral. These events also raised questions about the use of violence in both attacking and defending the state, with the younger generation particularly concerned at the levels of violence the state seemed prepared to use to silence its critics.

In direct response to this autumn of violence a group of the new directors – including Alf Brustellin, Fassbinder, Kluge, Maximiliane Mainka, Edgar

Reitz, Katja Ruppé, Hans Peter Cloos, Bernhard Sinkel, and Schlöndorff – collectively made *Germany in Autumn* (*Deutschland im Herbst*, 1978). An attempt to both document and comment upon the events of autumn 1977, the film was also meant to be a way of countering the news blackout at the time and to offer an alternative version of events to the official one. A formally experimental film, *Germany in Autumn* opens with documentary footage of Schleyer's state funeral, with a voice-over reading extracts from a letter he wrote to his son while in captivity. This is followed by various fictional or staged sequences, intercut with archive footage from German history, an interview with Horst Mahler (thought to be a co-founder of the RAF) from his prison cell, and concludes with documentary footage of the terrorists' funeral and short interviews with those involved in its arrangement.

Some segments of the film are clearly delineated, such as the one made by Fassbinder which comes immediately after the opening footage of the Schleyer funeral. In this, the most direct and brutal of the contributions, Fassbinder films a discussion he has with his mother, Lilo Eder, in which she explains she has been called a 'sympathiser' for merely defending Böll and likens the current repressive political climate to the Nazi era. She also argues that democracy is inadequate to deal with the situation unleashed by the rise of urban terrorism and suggests what is needed is 'some kind of authoritarian ruler who is really good and proper'. Although Fassbinder expresses fear of reprisals for his own left-wing views, he disagrees with his mother's viewpoint, arguing that it is precisely at times of crisis that democracy has to prove itself. However, he intercuts this discussion with staged scenes in his flat with his lover Armin, who declares all the terrorists should be shot and the plane at Mogadishu blown up. Fassbinder responds by openly bullying Armin, treating him like his servant, while criticising the state's use of violence to combat violence. His hypocritical behaviour suggests that the issue of dealing with terrorism may not be as straightforward as either his mother or Armin seem to think.

Similarly, Schlöndorff's contribution, a collaboration with Böll, is a separate short drama about the cancellation of a television broadcast of Sophocles' *Antigone*. The programme is screened at a meeting between television executives and the scriptwriters, where they discuss the play's themes of violence and resistance to the state, and decide it is too topical and inflammatory, and that it should be 'put on ice for calmer times'.

Thus the film conveys a sense of the repressive climate and hysteria that had developed in Germany during the 1970s as a result of the state response to terrorism. Indeed, in the footage of the terrorists' funeral many of those attending have covered their faces for fear of being recognised. At the same time, it also conveys the reality of the actual violence on both sides. In Schleyer's letter to his son after he had been kidnapped, quoted at the beginning of the film, he states 'we know there is no more protection against the meticulous, relentless work of the RAF ... peace will not be achieved quickly', while towards the end of the film we see a stark and horrifying image of Gudrun Ensslin's corpse laid out in a coffin.

Other contributions to *Germany in Autumn* are less clearly structured than the Fassbinder and Schlöndorff sequences, giving the film an episodic and at times disjointed quality. Kluge, for instance, creates the figure of Gabi Teichert, a history teacher who takes a spade out into the woods and tries to literally dig for the essence of German history. A voice-over explains that since 1977 she has been in some doubt about what to teach and is trying to get things in perspective. But rather than featuring in a short finite drama, she appears on various occasions in the course of the film, continuing her search for German history in different locations. And throughout the film, archive footage of violent acts and other funerals from German history is intercut, such as the execution of Rosa Luxemburg, Rommel's state funeral, and the assassination of the King of Serbia.

Hence the film also links contemporary events and violence with Germany's past, and this link is made evident at the very beginning of the film. A few minutes in, there is a subtitle: 'When atrocity reaches a certain point, it no longer matters who initiated it; it only matters that it should stop.' The statement immediately seems an appropriate comment on the situation in 1977, but it is dated 8 April 1945. Furthermore, it is credited to a 'Frau Wilde, mother of five', which also highlights how families can be touched by political events.[1] Indeed, Thomas Elsaesser has described the film as being 'about fathers and sons, mothers and sons, symbolic fathers and physical fathers, political fathers and rebellious children'

(1989: 260). Thus the film also links the private and personal with the public and the political. This is of course also evident in Fassbinder's contribution, with the inclusion of his mother and his relationship with Armin as integral to his own response to the events of 1977. The extent to which this personal element is 'fictionalised' is unclear – indeed Lilo Eder later said that Fassbinder had distorted her words in the process of editing (Thomsen 1997: 253) – but it nevertheless highlights its relationship with the political.

Unlike *The Lost Honour of Katharina Blum*, the film had a more limited impact on the wider public. In a sense this is not surprising, given its experimental form, but responses to it were also more universally negative than with other New German Cinema films. When it was premiered at the 1978 Berlin Film Festival, the Right condemned it because it was more critical of the anti-terrorist measures than of the actual terrorist actions, while the Left criticised it for not detailing the political struggle more clearly. However, it is nevertheless a significant film since it heralded the start of a process of remembering and mourning the past – in particular the Nazi past – often through an examination of personal experiences and stories, that was to be pursued in a number of other New German Cinema films.

Remembering the past

After the war there had been a desire to forget the Nazi past, and during the 1950s it had simply not been a subject for public discussion. As Margarethe von Trotta has observed: 'We felt that there was a past of which we were guilty as a nation but we weren't told about in school. If you asked questions, you didn't get answers' (quoted in Bergman 1984: 47). During the late 1970s, however, for a number of reasons the Germans finally began to 'remember' and deal with their recent history. The events of autumn 1977 were certainly a significant contributing factor, but the broadcast of the eight-hour-long American television series *Holocaust* on West German television in 1979 also played a major role in precipitating this 'remembering' process.

As the first major commercial 'film' to deal with the persecution of the Jews during the Nazi era, it was bound to elicit a strong response in West

Germany. In contrast to *Germany in Autumn*, *Holocaust* uses a classical realist narrative to tell the story of the fictional Jewish Weiss family. Their private lives and love stories are intermeshed with real historical events to chart the wider reality of the systematic persecution and annihilation of the German Jews between 1933 and 1945. Through their personal stories we learn about the Nuremberg Laws, *Kristallnacht*, the euthanasia programme, and the concentration camps. Full of drama and romance, loyalty and betrayal, the series – starring Meryl Streep and James Woods, and broadcast in four parts – attracted approximately 120 million viewers when it was broadcast in the US in 1978 and was sold to 50 countries worldwide, including West Germany, during that year.

On the one hand, many Germans found the series akin to soap opera and criticised it for the perceived trivialisation of German history. A survivor of Auschwitz declared: 'Untrue, offensive, cheap: as a television production, the film is an insult to those who perished and to those who survived. In spite of its name, this "docu-drama" is not about what some of us remember as the Holocaust' (quoted in Kaes 1989: 28). At the same time, however, according to Anton Kaes, *Holocaust* achieved enormously high viewing figures and elicited a tremendous direct response: over 20 million West Germans – which means 50 per cent of the adult population – watched *Holocaust* and the television station that broadcast it received over 30,000 phone calls and thousands of letters (Kaes 1989: 30). In the wake of its screening, various radio stations, magazines and newspapers addressed the issue of war crimes, and people began to share their experiences and memories of the Nazi era, even admitting to having collaborated in the discrimination against the Jews by turning a blind eye to what was happening. Such was the enormity of the impact of screening *Holocaust* in West Germany that Heinz Höhne writing for *Der Spiegel* observed:

> An American television series, made in a trivial style, produced more for commercial than for moral reasons, more for entertainment than for enlightenment, accomplished what hundreds of books, plays, films, and television programmes, thousands of documents, and all the concentration camp trials have failed to do in more than

three decades since the end of the war: to inform Germans about
crimes against Jews committed in their name so that millions were
emotionally touched and moved. (in Kaes 1989: 30–1)

Thus, it was as if for the first time West Germans had finally dared to really
confront their own past. Combined with the events of autumn 1977, the
screening of *Holocaust* not only triggered a widespread interest in the
German past, but helped initiate the process of 'remembering' that past
and – unsurprisingly perhaps – generated much debate about how history
should be represented on film. And by the early 1980s a number of New
German Cinema directors had endeavoured to explore the Nazi past in a
way that had not been attempted before. Indeed, at a press conference to
publicise *Germany in Autumn*, the contributing film-makers had already
declared that their future agenda was 'to concern ourselves with the
images of our country' (Brustellin *et al.* 1988: 132).

Some of the films that have been singled out for attention in this
connection are *Hitler, A Film From Germany* (*Hitler – ein Film aus Deutschland*,
1976–77) by Hans-Jürgen Syberberg, Fassbinder's *The Marriage of Maria
Braun* (*Die Ehe der Maria Braun*, 1978), Kluge's *The Patriot* (*Die Patriotin*,
1979), Helma Sanders-Brahms' *Germany, Pale Mother* (*Deutschland,
bleiche Mutter*, 1979–80) and Edgar Reitz's 16-hour television epic *Heimat*
(1984). Rather than being about historical events, some of these stylistically
very different films tried – at one level – to explore how the German people
had experienced the Hitler era as a lived reality.

To do this the films still tend to concentrate on the telling of personal
stories. For instance, Fassbinder's film follows one woman's struggle
to survive during the immediate post-war period when her husband at
first fails to return from the war and then goes to prison for a murder
she accidentally commits in his defence. But in complete contrast to
Holocaust, where the personal stories are used to dramatise real historical
events, the focus on personal stories in these films relegates the historical
reality to more of a backdrop – albeit an important one that helps shape
their lives – or in some cases is virtually excluded.

In Sanders-Brahms' film, *Germany, Pale Mother*, for instance, the
director looks back to her own childhood, the lives of her parents and

FIGURE 5 Lene walks to Berlin with her daughter in *Germany, Pale Mother* (1979–80)

their experiences of the 1950s. Predominantly narrative-based, the film shows her parents – Hans and Lene (played by Eva Mattes) – meeting in the 1930s, her father's experiences as a drafted soldier during the Second World War, how she and Lene survive on the home front, and the difficulties the family face in settling down to a peace-time existence. Unable to adjust to post-war life, Hans becomes increasing brutal towards his family, while Lene develops a facial paralysis and tries to commit suicide.

Although Sanders-Brahms drew on the experiences of other women who lived through the period to develop the film, it is presented as semi-autobiographical. Its status as a 'personal story' is also emphasised by the use of an intermittent directorial voice-over: the director makes herself overtly the narrator of her own story. And she uses the voice-over narration to recall clearly personal memories of her mother Lene. When the family house is completely destroyed in an air-raid, for instance, the voice-over remembers: 'With the end of the living room you became merry.' The film also dwells on the personal experiences of the young couple, rather than the historical reality they lived through or public events. For instance, when Hans and Lene marry, we are not shown the actual wedding, but only see them as they enter their new home – the domestic sphere – together for the first time, in their wedding clothes, and as they fumblingly and lovingly undress each other in their bedroom.

The historical reality of the Nazi regime under which they live is in evidence – via flags, uniformed officers, references to the 'Führer' and so on. As Lene and Hans undress each other on their wedding night, for instance, Lene comments that at least there is no picture of the Führer hanging over the marital bed. And at the beginning of the film the director draws attention to the existence of Nazism by stating in voice-over that although her parents' love story is 'happy, perfectly normal ... it happened at this particular time and in this country'. Nevertheless, Sanders-Brahms represents the wider reality as something in which the young couple have no interest and – importantly – over which they have no control. Their personal experiences are inevitably shaped by historical events but they are not represented as taking part in them. And this is apparent both at the narrative level and in the *mise-en-scène*.

At the narrative level, for instance, the young couple's domestic bliss is torn apart when Hans receives his call-up papers because he is not a party member, while his friend Ulrich who is a party member is allowed to remain on the home front. Hans does not want to fight, and when ordered to help kill a group of Polish peasants finds himself unable to do so because one of them resembles his wife (and is in fact also played by Eva Mattes). But he has no choice. In a similar vein, Lene finds herself unable to buy embroidery thread because the local Jewish-owned haberdashery store has been closed down. Thus the persecution of the Jews affects her life, but she has no interest in what has happened to the owners of the haberdashery store – and even seems surprised that the store is closed – she is only concerned to find the embroidery thread she needs.

These narrative concerns are echoed in the *mise-en-scène*. At the dance where Hans and Lene meet, an extremely large Nazi flag forms a backdrop, but Hans literally only has eyes for Lene and appears oblivious to the political regime under which he lives. On another occasion Lene hears noises outside in the street late at night and on looking out of her bedroom window sees her Jewish friend Rachel being taken away. The incident is filmed through the window from Lene's position inside the house. This has the effect of distancing her from what is happening, suggesting that it is something external to and not part of *her* life. Her experiences on the home front are also occasionally intercut with archive newsreel footage. For example, the scenes of Lene giving birth are intercut with aerial footage of a bomb-damaged city. The difference in film stock is, however, very noticeable and has the effect of suggesting that Lene's life and the war exist in separate spheres. While she experiences the effects of war – when, for instance, her house is bombed and reduced to a heap of rubble – the *mise-en-scène* positions her apart from historical events, as more of a neutral observer than a participant.

This does not mean that Sanders-Brahms considers her parents and people like them absolved of any responsibility for the atrocities that occurred during the Nazi era. On the contrary, she counts her parents among the many people who 'elected Hitler. Or perhaps didn't vote, but also didn't protest, or go underground, or join the resistance, or end up in concentration camps or emigrate' (Sanders-Brahms 1980: 9). But she does draw a distinction between actual lived reality and historical events and tries to show how for many Germans their everyday lives appeared to be quite separate from the wider political reality. While *Holocaust* represents the Hitler years purely in terms of the persecution of the Jews – implying that the worst excesses of Nazism constitute that period of

FIGURE 6 Director Edgar Reitz and cameraman Gernot Roll on the set of *Heimat* (1984)

German history – *Germany, Pale Mother* reveals another side to that history.

This distinction is also very apparent in Edgar Reitz's television epic *Heimat* (1984). Like Sanders-Brahms' film, *Heimat* is semi-autobiographical. Set in the Hunsrück region, a rural area in the southern part of the Rhineland – where Reitz himself was born – the epic 16-hour film traces through a chronological narrative the lives and fortunes of the inhabitants of the small fictional village of Schabbach from 1919 to 1982. Structured into 11 episodes and filmed in both colour and black and white, it revolves primarily around Maria who is 19 at the start of the film. In the course of the film she falls in love with and marries Paul Simon, has two sons, copes with Paul's desertion when he disappears off to America in 1928, lives through Nazism and the post-war reconstruction era, and eventually dies a lonely woman at the age of 82.

Heimat's relegation of historical events to a mere backdrop to the personal stories of the Schabbach villagers is very apparent in the nearly total exclusion of the persecution of the Jews – even though five of the 11 episodes deal with the Nazi era. Given the centrality of the Holocaust in received German history this seems incredible, and of course contrasts dramatically with the representation offered by the American series *Holocaust*, yet Schabbach is represented as an isolated rural environment, far removed from the 'outside world'. Some of the inhabitants do leave the confines of the village either temporarily or permanently – in addition to Paul Simon, Maria's brother-in-law Eduard spends some time in Berlin, for instance, where he meets his wife Lucie, and Apollonia who works in the local pub leaves to join the French father of her baby – but many remain, rarely if ever venturing beyond the village limits. Hence, it suggests that major historical events are only ever glimpsed from afar and experienced fleetingly and partially.

This is made explicit in a sequence in episode three, for instance, when three Nazi officers briefly visit Schabbach to have political discussions in 'undisturbed seclusion'. They conduct their talks in Eduard and Lucie's house, and a large number of villagers gather outside, gossiping about the identities of the officers and the number, size and colour of the motorbikes and cars that have transported the officers' entourage. Similarly inside, Lucie gossips to her husband about what the officers look like and what they said to her. The superficiality of this direct contact with the Nazi regime is reinforced through the way that parts of the scene are shot from Lucie and Eduard's perspective. As the officers prepare to leave, we see them peeking out from the kitchen through a partially open door, and as the officers walk down the corridor towards the kitchen they are filmed through the doorway so that we see only Eduard and Lucie's partial view of the departing Nazis – just as Lene is filmed in *Germany, Pale Mother* witnessing through a window her Jewish friend Rachel being taken away. Once the officers have passed the doorway, we are not shown them actually leaving the house, instead the camera stays on the empty corridor filmed from inside the kitchen – where Lucie and Eduard remain – through the kitchen doorway.

This view of German history offered by *Heimat* was given an authenticity through the involvement of the local population, who not only took acting roles, but supplied everyday objects for use in the film, and shared stories and anecdotes with Reitz which often found their way into the film. And the viewer response to the film when it was screened on German television in 1984 suggested that Reitz's stories and images about the Hunsrück region struck a very resonant chord among the German population. Due to its prime time screening slot, it attracted an average of 9 million viewers for each episode, and no fewer than 25 million West Germans saw at least one of the 11 episodes (Kaes 1989: 163). In the wake of its screening, Reitz received hundreds of letters from people telling him about their personal memories. And although Schabbach is a fictional place, it was a composite of four real Hunsrück villages and apparently produced such a strong impression of reality that tourists started to visit the region looking for it.

The concentration on personal stories in films like *Germany, Pale Mother* and *Heimat*, often to the virtual exclusion of political events, means that they act as a powerful counter-balance to populist representations of German history – such as *Holocaust* – with their concentration on public figures and historical events. The films imply that they are revealing a previously marginalised or unacknowledged reality. And response to *Heimat* in particular suggests that they certainly offered a point of recognition for Germans that had previously not existed. Thus, it is possible to argue that the process of remembering the past and trying to represent it as a lived reality was inextricably linked to addressing questions of German identity.

This is particularly apparent in Reitz's television series through its very deliberate tapping of the powerful German concept of 'Heimat'. The term translates loosely as 'homeland' and is closely associated with a rural environment – hence Reitz's choice of a village in the middle of nowhere. But it also embodies a sense of belonging and the idea of a place not yet attained but for which everyone yearns. It is usually linked to strong feelings and can be evocative of both hope and loss, in that it always implies a return to either real or imagined roots. Hence it is fundamentally tied up with a sense of identity and over the centuries has been appropriated by German nationalists to mobilise nationalist sentiments against perceived external foes, those who do not belong, outsiders, strangers and foreigners. And throughout Reitz's *Heimat*, there is an underlying theme of 'belonging' constructed through references to and narrative elements revolving around its opposite: 'foreigners' who come to the village, those who live on its outskirts and hence do not properly belong, or inhabitants who return but have been marked in some way by their encounter with the outside world and no longer fit in. Karl Glasisch, for instance, is a young man who like Paul Simon has returned from the war, but is described as having 'a skin infection from poison gas'. As a result he has 'scabby' hands and is shunned by many of the other villagers.

Of course, Reitz's choice of title also draws on the *Heimatfilm* genre and a pre-existing nineteenth-century literary genre of novels and dramas, which typically set up a contrast between the supposed purity, idyll, moral order and stable social hierarchy of the rural world on the one hand, and the corruption, sin, decay and decadence of city life on the other. The nineteenth-century novels are considered to have performed an escapist or wish-fulfilling function, in that they are thought to have been aimed at those people who, in the face of technological progress and the industrial revolution, were confronted with the need to migrate from the countryside into the cities in search of work and consequently became part of a rootless urban population. That is, they had lost their physical 'Heimat', and their sense of 'Heimat' – and hence their identity – seemed threatened in a rapidly changing world. Thus, the novels satisfied a yearning for a lost stability and social order. Although the films vary quite considerably in their precise form and content and although the film genre has gone through various developmental stages, they nevertheless deal with the same kind of ideas and these are echoed in Reitz's *Heimat*. Early in episode one, for instance, Eduard reads out a newspaper report about Spartacists robbing passengers on a tram in Munich, to which one character responds that it is a good job there are no trams in Schabach and another declares she shall never go to a city. External elements do, however, intrude into Schabach – the naked body of an unknown dead women, for instance, is discovered in the surrounding woods in episode one, while technological progress comes in the form of the radio and brings news and voices from the outside world – reinforcing the contrast between the rural village idyll and the 'otherness' of the outside world.

But Reitz's television epic also seems to insist on or reaffirm the existence of 'Heimat', a place where one belongs, that one can return to. When Paul Simon returns from the First World War at the beginning of episode one, for instance, without a word, without even taking his coat off or first going inside his parents house, he immediately starts helping his father in his blacksmith's workshop as if he has never been away. By representing this sense of 'Heimat', of a place one can return to, where one belongs, it is possible to argue that the series is precisely giving expression to a need for 'Heimat', for a self-determined sense of identity that counters the representation of German history offered by a 'film' like *Holocaust*. And Reitz seems to self-consciously suggest this by including the words 'Made in Germany' as a subtitle to each episode.

While such films may expand our understanding of what it means to be German and may be a more accurate representation of how many Germans did actually experience Hitler's Third Reich, it is nevertheless difficult to ignore the fact that they thereby avoid any exploration of who should bear responsibility for the Nazi atrocities. Thus the films have also been viewed as 'revisionist' – that is, it has been suggested that they attempt to 'rewrite' German history in a manner that is more palatable to the Germans, 'to fit the atrocities of the Hitler period into a tolerable master narrative' (Kaes 1989: x). Although Sanders-Brahms had begun developing the idea of *Germany, Pale Mother* as early as 1976, for instance, it was widely 'read' as just such an attempt. In her defence, Sanders-Brahms has argued that the attempt to depict the actual lived reality of many Germans is not intended to be an excuse for their lack of opposition to the Nazi regime. Rather it is offered as a warning to her own generation against adopting a morally superior position when standing in judgement on their parents. She asserts: 'I don't live any differently to my parents, only in different times' (Sanders-Brahms 1980: 11). Thus, just as Fassbinder's contribution to *Germany in Autumn* suggests that the issues raised by terrorism are more complex than at first appears, Sanders-Brahms suggests that the same may be true with regard to dealing with the Nazi past.

American imperialism and popular culture

It is possible to argue that the Nazi era also bequeathed another legacy in addition to the repression of its memory and the debate over how German history should be represented. With the defeat of German fascism, the Allies took over the administration of Germany and carved up the nation and its capital city of Berlin into four zones of occupation. As the US came to dominate the Western sectors, they brought with them American culture in all shapes and forms. The trappings of American life became so common-place that film-maker Wim Wenders and others have referred to the 'Americanisation' of West Germany (Sandford 1981: 104). Indeed, in his film *Kings of the Road* (*Im Lauf der Zeit*, 1976) Wenders has one of the characters observe: 'The Yanks have colonised our subconscious.' Although this 'Americanisation' of West Germany was not entirely uncontested – there were attempts to construct a new German identity, cleansed of fascism (Fehrenbach 1995: 5) – at some levels it did seem to be welcomed. When Hollywood films reappeared in the cinemas, for instance, Germans literally flocked to see what they had been missing.

Also, on the whole, West Germans were well-disposed towards the Americans in the immediate post-war years. Not only had they been seen by many as saviours in 1945, but they assumed this role again three years later. As relations deteriorated between the Soviet Union and the three Western occupying powers, and once the division of the country into two separate German states began to become a reality, Berlin became an area of contestation. As it was geographically located in East Germany, the Soviets wanted to eject the Western Allies from their zones of occupation and incorporate the city fully into East Germany. But maintaining West Berlin as a free, democratic stronghold in the face of communism became highly symbolic to the West and had enormous propagandistic value. In 1948 the Soviets blockaded West Berlin, closing off road, rail and river access to the city, and cutting off coal and electricity supplies, in an attempt to force the Western Allies to abandon the city. Instead, they launched a major airlift campaign and kept the city supplied until the Soviets eventually backed down. Although other Western nations helped fly in coal and food to West Berlin, it was the US government that had actually organised the airlift and mobilised resources, most of which were in fact American. Their vital role in the airlift campaign meant that the Americans were viewed as the city's saviours by most West Germans and cemented good relations with the US in order to ensure their continued support and help in protecting West Berlin and the new Federal Republic.

Wenders has also pointed to additional reasons for the Germans so readily embracing American culture. In part it can be viewed as emanating from a basic distrust of their own culture, now heavily tainted by Nazi ideology: 'Never before and in no other country have images and language been abused so unscrupulously as here, never before and nowhere else have they been debased so deeply as vehicles to transmit lies' (1988: 128). At the same time, there was an accompanying desire to blot out the unpleasant memory of Nazism: 'The need to forget 20 years created a hole, and people tried to cover this ... by assimilating American culture' (in Sandford 1981: 104).

Thus, for the new generation of directors, all of whom had grown up in post-war Germany, American culture was very much part of everyday life. It is unsurprising therefore that a number of their films engage with various aspects of this experience. Several directors, for instance, highlighted the influence of Hollywood cinema by drawing on the conventions of American films while dealing with specifically German subject matter. Fassbinder, for instance, made three films which are all set in the criminal underworld of Munich but which also play with the conventions and plots of the Hollywood gangster genre: *Love is Colder Than Death* (*Liebe ist kälter als der Tod*, 1969), *Gods of the Plague* (*Götter der Pest*, 1970), and *The American Soldier* (*Der amerikanische Soldat*, 1970). Later, he also turned his attention to Hollywood melodramas, especially those directed by Douglas Sirk, such as *Written on the Wind* (1956) and *Imitation of Life* (1959). Sirk's films attracted critical praise in the 1970s for the way in which they could be read as exposing the underlying tensions present in 1950s American society. During the late 1970s and early 1980s Fassbinder made a number of films, such as *Lili Marleen* (1980) and *Lola* (1981) which drew on the style of Sirk's films and the conventions of melodrama to explore German society. Indeed, he declared that 'Sirk's been in everything I've done' (quoted in Bratton *et al.* 1994: 106). While this may be a typically excessive overstatement, it is evident in *Fear Eats the Soul* discussed earlier, which can be viewed as a remake of Sirk's *All That Heaven Allows* (1955). Sirk's original similarly deals with the relationship between an older woman (played by Jane Wyman) and a younger man (Rock Hudson) that meets with disapproval from her children. However, it is class difference in Sirk's film that complicates the relationship, rather than the racial difference and resulting racism that Fassbinder explores in his film and which gives it a specifically German slant. As Fassbinder argued in an article he wrote about Sirk: 'The idea is to make films as beautiful as America's, but which at the same time shift the content to other areas' (1975: 23).

However, by the time Wenders, Fassbinder and others were making these films, attitudes towards the American presence in West Germany – particularly among the younger generation – were becoming more ambivalent. As the student movement protested against America's involvement in Vietnam, it highlighted what many now began to perceive as America's equally imperialist role in the Federal Republic. While many of the New German Cinema films pay homage to American cinema and celebrate its achievements, they often also critique the country's imperialism.

This ambivalence towards the 'Americanisation' of West Germany is particularly evident in Wenders' film *The American Friend* (*Der amerikanische Freund*, 1977). Based on the Patricia Highsmith novel *Ripley's Game*, the film centres on a friendship that develops between Ripley (played by Dennis Hopper), a crooked American art-dealer living in Hamburg, and Jonathan (Bruno Ganz), a German picture framer suffering from a terminal illness. When Ripley and Jonathan meet for the first time at an auction, Jonathan's clear contempt for him offends Ripley. In retaliation, Ripley suggests Jonathan to a French underworld contact who is looking for an assassin. Initially dumbfounded by the suggestion that he carry out a contract killing, Jonathan is tricked into carrying out two murders in return for a sizeable payment so that he can leave his family well provided for after his death. His wife, however, wants nothing to do with the money, and due to the stress of his 'adventures' Jonathan dies prematurely.

The ambivalence towards America is expressed narratively in the relationship that develops between Ripley and Jonathan. The latter's dislike of Ripley and his shady dealings results in Ripley tricking Jonathan into thinking his illness is much worse than it is and that he will die in the near future. In order to provide for his family, Jonathan agrees to undertake the two assassinations. This can be read symbolically as signifying an antagonistic relationship between their respective countries. And Ripley's treatment of Jonathan, leading him into a life of crime and to an early death, implies any German dislike of America is totally justified. Other narrative details also suggest a deep mistrust of America's motives for remaining in Europe. Ripley is only in Hamburg in order to use the German art market to circulate forged paintings, and there is a suggestion through one of the murders that Jonathan commits that the Americans are making money out of the German porn industry. Thus the film seems to suggest that America is exploiting Germany for her own ends.

Yet Ripley has a conscience. The day before Jonathan is due to commit the second assassination he tries to get Jonathan to undertake work for him instead and they strike up a friendly conversation. When his distraction tactics fail, Ripley turns up unexpectedly on the train where the assassination is to take place to help Jonathan out and ends up committing the murder for him. As a result an uneasy bond and cameraderie develops between the two men, to the exclusion of the latter's wife. When Jonathan eventually finds out why Ripley tricked him in the first place, he is amused rather than angry, continues to enjoy Ripley's company, and is able to see the funny side of their predicament.

However, the film also clearly owes much to Hollywood cinema. Ripley dresses, behaves and even talks like the hero from a latter-day western. For example, he frequently sports a cowboy hat – indeed Ripley's American forger draws attention to it by asking if he wears it in Hamburg, and Ripley responds by asking 'what's wrong with a cowboy in Hamburg?' And when

Ripley finds someone apparently breaking into his house, he creeps up behind them and says: 'Freeze, mister, I gotta gun.' The final section of the film also begins with a 'stake-out' at Ripley's place, followed by a 'shoot-out' between him and Jonathan on the one hand and the underworld fraternity they have become embroiled with on the other. In addition to the casting of Dennis Hopper, American directors Samuel Fuller and Nicholas Ray both have cameo roles, while the second murder on board a train recalls scenes from two Hitchcock thrillers, *Strangers on a Train* (1951) and *North by Northwest* (1959) which both have key scenes that take place on a train. All these factors suggest a fascination on Wenders' part with American films. Yet again an ambivalence is apparent. The film makes it clear that both Ripley as 'a cowboy in Hamburg' and Jonathan as the reluctant assassin are acting out roles, roles that are amusing at times, but also ludicrous at others. The two men are clearly attracted to the excitement of those roles – as if they offer the possibility of entering the fictional worlds of American movies – but at the end of the film, Jonathan rejects the world Ripley has drawn him into by leaving Ripley stranded on a beach and driving off with his wife. Moreover, the roles that they 'play with' have serious consequences, resulting in a number of deaths, including Jonathan's own which leaves his wife a widow and his son fatherless.

Thus, at a number of levels, *The American Friend* can be viewed as giving expression to a love-hate relationship with the American presence and role in West German life. Other films, however, are more outrightly negative in their critique of America's cultural imperialism. Werner Herzog's *Stroszek* (1976), for instance, draws on the myth of the American Dream so frequently mediated by Hollywood films to explore the potentially disastrous effects of American ideology on alien cultures. Indeed, Herzog has asserted there is such strong domination of Western Europe by American culture and American films that, 'for me, it was particularly important to define my position about this country and its culture, and that's one of the major reasons I made *Stroszek*' (quoted in Corrigan, 1994: 128).

The film revolves around Bruno Stroszek, released from prison at the beginning of the film after completing a two-and-a-half year sentence. On his way back to the flat that his elderly neighbour Scheitz has kept for him, he meets up with Eva, a prostitute who is being badly treated by her two pimps. Bruno takes her back to stay at his place, where Scheitz tells them that he has been invited to go and join his nephew, Clayton, in the US. Pursued by her pimps, Eva suggests they leave Berlin for America with Scheitz. When the three of them arrive in New York they drive to Wisconsin where Clayton lives in a desolate rural town called Railroad Flats. Living in a huge mobile home, Bruno goes to work as a mechanic in Clayton's garage and Eva gets a job as a waitress in a truck stop. Although things go well to start with, they gradually fall behind with their repayments on the mobile home and Eva starts working as a prostitute again to make up the shortfall. As their relationship deteriorates, however, Eva leaves with a couple of truckers going to Vancouver and the mobile home is repossessed. Faced with nowhere to live and no money, Bruno and Scheitz hold up a barber's shop and use the little money they get to buy a frozen turkey at a shop across the road. While Scheitz is arrested, Bruno escapes in Clayton's breakdown truck to an Indian Reservation in North Carolina, where he rides up and down in a chair-lift with his turkey and a rifle.

Bruno and Eva are drawn to the US initially since it appears to present a safe haven from the dangers they encounter in Berlin. Eva's pimps repeatedly beat her up for not earning enough and start to rough Bruno up for looking after her. When they arrive in the US Bruno blows a bugle, one of his treasured possessions, just as he did when he was released from prison, suggesting he is similarly going to freedom. As they settle into their mobile home, we also see several shots of Bruno and Eva embracing, talking or doing domestic chores, which suggests their new lives have given them the chance to build a caring and supportive relationship.

However, as it becomes apparent to Bruno that they cannot afford their mobile home, he becomes increasingly disillusioned. He declares he thought they could get rich quick, but begins to realise things are not so different from the world they left behind in Germany. No one kicks him physically in America as they did in Berlin, he says, but they do so spiritually. As Eva returns to prostitution to earn more money, their relationship also suffers, and the shots of them framed together in domestic harmony are replaced by shots of them in separate bedrooms. Although Berlin and Railroad Flats are very different places, the images of both are stark and

FIGURE 7 Eva and Bruno share a home together in *Stroszek* (1976)

uninviting – Berlin with its world of bars, pimps and run-down courtyards, and Railroad Flats with its flat desolate landscape and deserted rail tracks. And this unpromising sense of place is emphasised through a very slow-moving narrative, which incorporates little traditional 'action'. The film thereby suggests a futile circularity – no matter what Bruno does, he ends up back where he began, and this is powerfully conveyed through the visual images at the end of the film. Ditching Clayton's breakdown truck, Bruno locks the steering wheel so that we watch it ceaselessly going round in circles until it burst into flames, while Bruno is shown riding endlessly up and down on the chair-lift.

But America is shown to be far more destructive than their native Germany. At least in Berlin, Bruno had his own flat, filled with musical instruments that he played and lovingly looked after. He was also part of a community: he had friends and neighbours and was greeted as a regular in his local bar. And when he bumps into Eva on leaving prison, he proudly announces: 'I am starting a new life today.' Falling prey to the myth of the

American Dream, however, Bruno expects things to be both easier and better in the US. Instead, he becomes isolated in the alien environment, loses a home which was never really his, is forced back into a life of crime, and ends up with nothing but a frozen turkey and nowhere to go. What little dignity, pride and hope he once possessed have been entirely lost. As we watch Clayton's breakdown truck in flames at the end of the film, we hear a gunshot and the camera pans across to the chair-lift. As we do not see Bruno, we are left to assume he has committed suicide. Thus, American culture with its continual propagation of the American Dream is shown to offer false promise and hope. Rather than being a land of freedom and opportunity, America is represented as isolating and destroying those who do not belong.

Both films convey a sense of Germans 'who get caught up in things bigger than they can handle' (Elsaesser 1989: 103), and those 'things' emanate from America. Jonathan is drawn unwittingly into an underworld of crime linked to American involvement in the German porn industry that is acted out like an American gangster-cum-cowboy movie and leads to his untimely death, while Bruno's naïve and idealistic vision of a better future in America does not survive the economic realities of living there. In both cases there are also parallels with the relationship between the German film industry and Hollywood, pointing to the latter's detrimental effect on the former. Indeed, Elsaesser asserts this is intentional in Wenders' film (*ibid.*), but given Herzog's reasons for making *Stroszek* it is an equally appropriate reading of his film. By 1978 West Germany was Hollywood's second largest export market – grossing US$51.9 million – while the German industry's share of its own home market had sunk to 8 per cent (Elsaesser 1989: 36). Thus, despite the specifically German subject matter of the films by the new directors, it is as if the Germans are fighting a losing battle to assert their own cultural identity against the global power of America.

Feminism, the authentic experience of women and German history

Just as the 'American experience' had an enormous impact on West German film-making, so too did the emergence of the women's movement.

Although women film-makers initially suffered from considerable levels of discrimination, which meant they often did not break through into feature film direction until the late 1970s, the influence of the women's movement eventually gave rise to a vibrant women's cinema as part of the New German Cinema. In fact, such was its impact that a number of male directors also turned to women's issues in their work. In 1971, for instance, Fassbinder made *The Bitter Tears of Petra von Kant* (*Die bitteren Tränen der Petra von Kant*) about a lesbian relationship, while Kluge addressed the subject of abortion in his film *Occasional Work of a Female Slave* (*Gelegenheitsarbeit einer Sklavin*, 1973).

The main impetus for the women's movement came from the student protest movement discussed earlier. Although the student movement was concerned with bringing about social change, its male leaders failed to acknowledge the oppression of women. Eventually, student film-maker Helke Sander delivered a stinging attack on her male colleagues during the 1968 Socialist German Students Union annual conference, and in the wake of her speech women's groups began to be set up throughout the country to campaign for women's rights. Although it took several years to gain momentum, the growing women's movement gradually raised awareness of and campaigned for political reform around such issues as childcare, abortion, women's health, violence against women, and sex discrimination in the workplace, and also gave rise to a women's counterculture.

Some feminist activists also drew attention to the way in which women have so often been excluded from the public domain, and thus their stories are rarely told, their experiences left unacknowledged. Although relatively few women film-makers actively participated in the women's movement, its consciousness-raising aims fostered a new women's cinema that was concerned with representing the authentic experiences of women. Indeed, as Elsaesser has asserted, by the 1980s West Germany had 'proportionally more women film-makers than any other film-producing country' (1989: 185). The majority of films that made up this new women's cinema explored or were based on the lives of actual women. Several film-makers simply turned their cameras on women in their own circle of friends and acquaintances to produce imaginative and experimental documentaries.

FIGURE 8 Helke Sander as single working mother Edda in *Redupers* (1977)

For example, in her film *A Thoroughly Demoralized Girl* (*Ein ganz und gar verwahrlostes Mädchen*, 1977), Jutta Brückner documents a day in the life of her friend Rita Rischak and her attempts to improve herself, while Elfi Mikesch made *I Often Think of Hawaii* (*Ich denke oft an Hawaii*, 1978) about her neighbour Ruth, a deserted wife and mother of two. Other films – such as *The Second Awakening of Christa Klages* and *The German Sisters* by Margarethe von Trotta – were, as mentioned above, based on the documented lives of real women.

However, some directors turned to their own experiences and produced semi-autobiographical feature films, such as Sanders-Brahms' *Germany, Pale Mother*, discussed earlier. Other examples are Helke Sander's *The All-round Reduced Personality – Redupers* (*Die allseitig reduzierte Persönlichkeit*, 1977), Jutta Brückner's *Years of Hunger* (*Hungerjahre*, 1980), Jeanine Meerapfel's *Malou* (1980) and Marianne Rosenbaum's

Peppermint Freedom (*Peppermint Frieden*, 1983). Although each film adopts a different approach to its subject matter, in many of them the directors – like Sanders-Brahms – look back to their childhoods, their experiences of growing up in the 1950s and the lives of their parents.

Others, however, are more contemporary. In *Redupers*, for instance, Sander explores her own experiences of being a working single mother. Made in black and white, the film focuses on Edda Chiemnyjewski, a single mother and freelance photographer living in West Berlin. It revolves around her attempts to balance her commitments as a mother and a member of a women's photography collective with her need to earn a living. In a very episodic narrative, the film shows the various sides of her life. In some scenes we see her with her child, in others she is out taking photos which she subsequently tries to sell to newspapers, attending gallery openings, indulging in leisure pursuits, spending time with her boyfriend, or working on the project being undertaken by the photography collective. Throughout the film there is also an intermittent voice-over which draws attention to and comments upon the difficulties that Edda encounters in her everyday life.

Through the photography project, the film draws attention to the city of Berlin and our perceptions of it when it was a divided city. Whereas conventional wisdom suggested that East and West Berlin were very different due to the opposing political regimes which governed them, Edda's photos highlight similarities – her pictures show car owners, for instance, on both sides of the Wall diligently cleaning their cars,. and political slogans adorning buildings in both East (in the form of official banners) and West (in the form of graffiti). But Sander also uses the project to highlight some of the difficulties women like herself faced in their professional lives. For instance, the women's photography collective only receive funding for their project because it is assumed they will produce work that deals with women's issues. And they are given less money than the funders budgeted for because as women 'they will be glad to get anything at all'. Made at a time when feminism had become 'fashionable', the film shows the funders expressing surprise and disappointment that the final project is not feminist in content. Having fought long and hard to get women's issues recognised, Sander found that she and other women were being ghettoised as feminist film-makers, expected to deal with women's issues in their work, and finding it difficult to access larger budgets.

The parallels in the film with Sander's own well-documented experiences of trying to combine her professional activity as a film-maker with her role as a single mother are also unmistakable. In the journal *Frauen und Film* (*Women and Film*) – which she founded in 1974 – Sander wrote extensively about the problems of being a working mother, as well as discrimination against women in the workplace. Moreover, as if to underline the autobiographical nature of the film, Sander herself plays the central protagonist, and an important dimension of the film is its acknowledgement of that double role that so many women undertake.

Since childcare was an aspect of women's lives all too frequently excluded from the mass media, Sander foregrounds Edda's role as a mother. In the opening scenes, for instance, Edda is shown getting ready to leave for work, picking up her young daughter as she does so to say goodbye. She hands the child over to her flatmate-cum-childminder, but the girl clings on to Edda's scarf and refuses to let go. In despair Edda takes the scarf off and leaves it dangling in her daughter's hand as she rushes out of the door. The position of this scene at the beginning of the film means that one of the first things we learn about Edda is that she is a mother. Its composition – mother and daughter in a tug-of-war – also emphasises how Edda's role as wage-earner conflicts with that of mother. This combination makes the scene very powerful and creates a lasting impression. Although the child is subsequently absent during whole sections of the film, *Redupers* intermittently includes reminders of the dual role of many women: as they work on their photography project on a Sunday morning, one character complains that one or another of them always has a child with them, while later another character interrupts their work in order to collect her child. Consequently, it is impossible as a viewer to forget what employers so frequently want to ignore – that women are often mothers as well as workers.

This desire to put on screen those aspects of women's lives that have usually been marginalised by or excluded from mainstream cinema can be seen time and again in the New German Cinema films made by women. Although *Germany, Pale Mother*, for instance, can be read as a film concerned with 'remembering' the Nazi past, it does so primarily through an exploration of the life of the director's mother, Lene. An interesting aspect of the film is its attention to details of Lene's experience that have been excluded from more conventional depictions of the era. For instance, when Lene's house is destroyed in an air-raid, she sets off on foot to seek shelter with her Berlin relatives. As we see her walking briskly and resolutely along a rubble-strewn street, what the voice-over narration points out is that she has to undertake this journey wearing high heels. And when she arrives at her relatives in Berlin, Sanders-Brahms includes a scene of Lene having a bath with her young daughter. Contrary to the usual eroticisation of the female body in mainstream cinema and its presentation as sexual spectacle, Lene is filmed from behind in order to playdown her nakedness and draw attention to the pleasure mother and daughter share in a moment of physical closeness.

In *Years of Hunger*, Jutta Brückner graphically depicts the moment a young 13-year-old girl gets her first period. At the beginning of the film, the young female protagonist is shown sitting on a toilet in the family bathroom. As she goes to pull up her knickers, she notices a blood stain on them. She gets a towel, wipes herself and then goes to her mother in a state of confusion, saying she is ill. Such aspects of women's reality have not, of course, been totally excluded from mainstream cinema: a girl's discovery of her first menstrual blood forms the opening sequence to Brian de Palma's *Carrie* (1976), for example. But in the context of de Palma's horror film the onset of menstruation serves as evidence of woman's impurity and ultimately leads to the destruction of a whole community, rather than being represented as part of women's authentic experience.

These films, with their concern to put on screen the authentic experiences of women, produced a cinema which offered women viewers a recognisable representation of themselves and their lives. Individual experiences obviously can and do differ according to race, age, class and so on, but the response these films met with suggests that some experiences can transcend such boundaries. Brückner, for instance, was surprised at the response that *Years of Hunger* elicited outside of Germany, since she felt the film was culturally specific. It focuses on a teenage girl, Ursula, growing up in the 1950s in a divided Germany. She becomes totally alienated from her own body due to the restrictive values espoused by those around her, and finally attempts suicide. Yet Brückner was repeatedly told by women from different countries, from totally different societies – such as Egypt – and from different generations to herself, how the film had reminded them of their own adolescence. And she made sense of this response to her film through a concept she termed 'collective gestures'. As she explains:

> There are certain ways of hiding one's feelings, certain types of inhibition ... for instance, in the scene where the daughter comes home after her accordion class, and a boy has asked her out. The daughter pulls her nightdress over her head before she undresses, just like her mother does, because right at that moment she's ashamed to undress in front of her mother. And then when the mother sits by her daughter's bed and strokes her hand over the quilt because she can't stroke the child itself any more, and doesn't want to, because suddenly a barrier has grown up between them. Obviously these are gestures which every woman knows: even if they didn't happen *exactly* like that, women can still remember how it *did* happen for them. (in Harbord 1981–82: 52)

Thus, without necessarily intending to, the films functioned as implicit explorations of women's shared or collective experiences. And this aspect of women's film production also attracted the attention of male viewers. Of *Redupers*, a male film critic observed:

> Helke Sander has not only succeeded in offering an impressively characterised portrait of the reduced city of Berlin, she has also managed to frame her own situation as author, *the situation of many professional women* in images and scenes against which men currently have shamefully little to say. (in Knight 1992: 89–90, my emphasis)

In some cases, male viewers even identified with the situation of the female protagonist. Again with regard to *Redupers*, Philip Hayward has stressed that: 'For me the film ... transcended its (very important) gender specific and made *me* (as a male) identify with the human predicament of the character and her social situation. I found the film really affecting' (in Knight 1992: 183–4). And in discussing *Years of Hunger* Jutta Brückner has asserted: 'A lot of men have told me they identify with Ursula, too. Well, her problem is that she doesn't want to be forced into a classic gender role' (in Harbord 1981–82: 52). This ability to represent contemporary collective experiences through an individual protagonist was singled out as a specific strength of women's film-making in West Germany. Although the films – like those by their male colleagues – were made within a national context, this aspect also gave them an obvious significance beyond that of a merely national cinema 'movement'.

But in turning to their own lives, women film-makers almost inevitably confronted questions of German history. This is evident in Sanders-Brahms' *Germany, Pale Mother*, Brückner's *Years of Hunger*, and again, through its focus on the divided city of Berlin, in Sander's *Redupers*. By examining those aspects of women's lives that have been marginalised by the mass media within the context of German history, however, much women's film-making necessarily called into question dominant ways of looking at things. In *Redupers*, for instance, Edda highlights the similarities rather than the differences between East and West Berlin through her photographs, and later also points out that the dominant perception is that it is the East Germans who are 'walled in', trapped inside their country, yet any map shows that it is the West Berliners who are surrounded by a wall. In a similar vein, *Germany, Pale Mother* reverses the dominant perceptions of war and peace-time. Lene experiences the war as a time of freedom from the oppression that women suffer at the hands of men, whereas peace-time brings the violent re-imposition of patriarchal order. As already mentioned, when Lene's house is destroyed in an air-raid, she becomes 'merry'. But when Lene develops a disfiguring facial paralysis after the war, Hans takes her to see a (male) dentist who insists that the only course of action is to extract Lene's teeth. Without consulting Lene and ignoring her visible distress, Hans authorises the dentist to go ahead with the operation. As Sanders-Brahms observes in voice-over: 'The stones we cleared away were used to build houses which were worse than before

... That was the return of the livings rooms. Then the war began inside, once there was peace outside.'

This issue of how we perceive and remember the past is a central theme in Claudia von Alemann's *Blind Spot* (*Die Reise Nach Lyon*, 1980). Through an episodic narrative, the film focuses on contemporary historian Elisabeth Falusy, who is researching the life and work of Flora Tristan, the largely forgotten nineteenth-century socialist and feminist. However, all her conventional library and archive research has left her dissatisfied, and she travels from her native Germany to Lyon, where Tristan spent some time, in order to try and find traces of her. Although Elisabeth's voice-over fills in a few details about Tristan's life, the film does not offer a conventional historical reconstruction of Tristan's life. Instead, the first half of the film shows how Elisabeth tries a number of different ways to search for evidence of Tristan only to find that the past is in fact highly elusive.

For instance, Elisabeth looks for the street in Lyon where a close friend of Tristan's had lived. Although she finds the street, its name has changed and no one can tell her where the house of Tristan's friend had been. Similarly she locates the hotel where Tristan stayed, but finds it is now a cinema showing karate movies. Adopting another tack, Elisabeth goes to an antiquarian bookshop and asks to see etchings of Lyon from the mid-nineteenth century. The bookseller has, however, lost a folder of etchings and consequently has only very few to show Elisabeth. Of the few she has, several are of a particular square in Lyon, but they all show the same view because – so the bookseller explains – there was less to see in the opposite view. Others depict workshops from the period, which Elisabeth remarks seem relatively large. But according to the bookseller, etchings – especially from that period – are not very accurate.

Thus the film foregrounds the way in which much of the past literally vanishes. In doing so, it calls into question the notion of historical truth and the possibility of historical reconstruction. From this perspective, it is possible to argue that the debate about how to represent Germany's past, about whether films like *Germany, Pale Mother* and *Heimat* are 'revisionist' is unproductive (although it is obviously an important debate in other contexts). In the second half of *Blind Spot*, Elisabeth explores the use of sound as a way of connecting and identifying with the past that she is seeking. But sound is also how Elisabeth remembers her own personal past: she uses a tape recorder to listen to a tape of her partner and their young daughter talking. Hence the film suggests that rather than one's personal past being separate from 'history', it can provide the means of accessing it. And it is possible to argue that this is precisely what Sanders-Brahms and Reitz were doing through their film projects, and that – given the previous repression of that past – the actual act of connecting with it *in some way* is just as important as how it is represented.

Counter-myths of German identity

The above analyses do not of course represent an exhaustive or comprehensive discussion of the themes and issues addressed by New German Cinema films. Other, equally important issues were taken up by various directors – for instance, gay and lesbian sexuality in the work of Fassbinder and Ulrike Ottinger, and the situation of the working class in the *Arbeiterfilme*. But the above discussion demonstrates how, by deliberately and self-consciously addressing contemporary issues within the institution of a national cinema, many of the New German Cinema films also inevitably explored and in turn raised questions about 'being German' in the post-war era – that is, about German identity. Indeed, cinema and television fictions are sites where a sense of national identity is constructed and articulated, and, as noted earlier, this is a shared characteristic of art cinema films in particular. Moreover, the subsidy system had been developed in part precisely to promote German culture both at home and abroad as a manifestation of German identity.

As a number of film and cultural theorists have argued, national and cultural identities are not stable or pre-existing, they are constantly in the *process* of being formed (Hurd 1984, Bhabha 1990, Andersen 1991, Petrie 1992). Drawing on the work of Homi Bhabha and Frantz Fanon, John Caughie has described it as something which is always being performed in the present and therefore never actually becomes, but is always on the point of *just* becoming:

> The emphasis [Bhabha] and Fanon put on the *'just'* refers to
> the liminality of a national culture, to its place on the threshold
> of enunciation, its shape sensed but never grasped in a single
> gesture, an identity which always seems about to be but never is,
> never achieves the stability which can be looked back on. (Caughie
> 1992: 36)

This means our sense of national identity can and does change over time.
This idea of national identity as a continual process is very similar to the
concept of myth in communication studies, which can be defined as any
means by which a society in some way makes sense of, understands,
organises, or comes to terms with itself.[2] Myths circulate through
repetition, through being continually told and retold, articulated and
rearticulated – be that through storytelling, through the mass media, by
replicating family relations and social practices or performing rituals – and
this is precisely how they fulfil their role. But irrespective of how myths
are physically circulated, any myth will only continue to be 'retold' for as
long as it is deemed relevant to the society that produces it: it is its very
relevance that perpetuates it. Thus, just as our sense of national identity
is unstable, no myth is eternal, fixed or stable for all time, but exists in
a dynamic relationship to the society which produces it, and myths will
change or disappear – even recur or resurface at a later time – as that
society's needs and values also change. At the same time, no myth is
universal in a culture – instead there will be both dominant myths and
counter-myths.

Hence the concept and articulation of national identity can be viewed
as a form of mythic narrative – it is a society talking to itself about itself.
While the 1950s film mentioned at the beginning of this chapter, *The
Fisherwoman from Lake Constance*, appeared to be 'escapist', it can
nevertheless be viewed as dealing with ideas that were relevant and
important to the German population in the immediate post-war period.
Similarly, the New German Cinema films discussed above were not
merely offering images and representations of contemporary reality, they
were working through ideas central to that reality. And in doing so, the
films from both eras were effectively exploring the experience of being

German during the periods in which the films were produced. Whereas in the 1950s this meant trying to 'escape' or deny the past, from the late 1960s through to the early 1980s it frequently meant confronting that past. Hence the films from the two different eras were articulating very different ideas about what it meant to be German. The 'escapist' films of the 1950s can be viewed as articulating a dominant myth of German identity, while the significance of many of the New German Cinema films lies in the fact that they mark the emergence of a number of counter-myths about 'being German' in the post-war era.

Helke Sander, for instance, makes this explicit in *Redupers*, by having Edda make her observations about the similarities – rather than the conventionally assumed differences – between East and West and about how it is the West Berliners rather than the East Germans who are walled in. In other films it is the image of the Federal Republic that comes under scrutiny. Its status as a political democracy is shaken by suggestions of prevailing fascist tendencies in *Fear Eats the Soul* and *Shirin's Wedding*, while the state is exposed as repressive and failing to protect the rights of the individual in *The Lost Honour of Katharina Blum* and *Germany in Autumn*. The usual concern with the documented public events of history is replaced with a focus on the personal or the actual lived experiences of 'ordinary' people in *Blind Spot, Germany, Pale Mother* and *Heimat*, which implicitly if not explicitly questions the centrality of the Holocaust in recent German history. And the idea of American culture being welcomed as a means of obliterating the memory of Nazism is countered by an exploration of the destructive effects of American cultural imperialism in *The American Friend* and *Stroszek*.

The issue of what it meant to be German in the post-war era was particularly apparent in the so-called 'Historians' Debate' that flared up in West Germany in 1986. The debate began with an article by Jürgen Habermas which attacked what he considered to be the 'apologist tendencies in German contemporary historiography' (quoted in Kaes 1989: 222) with regard to the origin and legacy of Auschwitz.[3] In particular Habermas was responding to a book by Andreas Hillgruber and an article by Ernst Nolte that tried to relativise the annihilation of the Jews under Hitler. Hillgruber, for instance, compared the defeat of the German army on the Eastern front in 1944–45 with the Holocaust. However, Habermas' article triggered off a widespread and bitter discussion among West German historians over the meaning and representation of German history. The New German Cinema films obviously address the more widely shared experiences of racism, intolerance, American cultural imperialism, the power of the mass media, and the marginalisation of women's experiences – giving them a relevance that extends beyond national boundaries. But Habermas' subsequent description of the Historians' Debate seems equally appropriate to the New German Cinema films: that they can be understood as part of a 'debate over the self-understanding of the Federal Republic' (in Torpey: 9).

And the fact of the films' existence suggests that the issue of national identity was of particular importance to Germans during the 1970s and early 1980s. Whilst a number of factors – which are addressed in chapter 3 – contributed to the demise of the New German Cinema, if we view the articulation of national identity as a form of mythic narrative, that demise can also be viewed as stemming in part from a decline in the relevance of the country's internal debate about its own identity to the population's contemporary reality.

3   DEMISE: INTO A NEW ERA

Sponsorship or censorship?

Although the New German Cinema met with international critical acclaim, it did not enjoy wide commercial success. As a result it remained dependent on public money for its existence and hence – contrary to the demands of the Oberhausen Manifesto – did not achieve the desired freedom from vested interests. State support may have helped produce a 'quality' national cinema, but it also shaped the nature of that cinema. It gradually diminished the breadth and diversity of it through political and artistic censorship and in the long run contributed to its demise. Such censorship was of course not new and had already occurred in the 1950s when tax concessions had first been tied into quality ratings. But as the new cinema became increasingly dependent on state support, it was increasingly difficult for projects that did not meet certain funding criteria to obtain support. A tendency to tailor funding applications to meet those criteria consequently became virtually unavoidable.

Although the funding agencies promoted film as an art form, for instance, the economic rationale underlying their guidelines often determined whether funds were awarded or not. In 1978 Wilhelm Roth commented on his work with the FFA project commission, observing that 'the main discussion that takes place ... is always about whether or not the film will be successful at the box-office' (in Knight 1992: 37). In its early days, the new cinema had incorporated documentary and formally experimental work alongside episodic narrative and more conventional feature films. The early films of a number of directors have, for instance, been characterised by their complete rejection of narrative cinema:

> Young German films ... often bore little reference explicitly or implicitly to national or international film culture. The early films of Syberberg or Herzog, for instance, were to a remarkable degree objects *sui generis*, outside any recognizable tradition of film-making either commerical or avant garde. (Elsaesser 1989: 25)

However, as subsidy policy became more commercially orientated, film-makers shunning traditional narrative forms began to experience difficulty in securing subsidies. Although in some cases directors still managed to obtain funding for more experimental work – such as Syberberg for his epic theatrical film *Hitler, A Film From Germany* (*Hitler – Ein Film aus Deutschland*, 1976–77) and Ulrike Ottinger, for her stylised portrait of a self-destructive lesbian alcoholic, *Ticket of No Return* (*Bildnis einer Trinkerin*, 1979) – the cinema became predominantly one of narrative-based feature films.

Projects that addressed politically sensitive issues or were socially critical also often failed to find funding. In 1975, for instance, Fassbinder submitted a proposal to the FFA entitled *The Garbage, The City and Death* (*Der Müll, die Stadt und der Tod*). Based on a Gerhard Zwerenz novel, Fassbinder had originally written it as a play which examined some of the negative aspects of capitalism. However, he was accused of anti-semitism and the play was never staged. The FFA felt that the racist implications persisted in the film project and refused it funding.

Even if a project was awarded funding this did not necessarily guarantee that the director or the resulting film would be free from censorship. A quality rating could be withheld which meant not only that a producer was not entitled to tax relief, but also that his or her film was required to gross a higher amount before he or she could qualify for an automatic FFA subsidy for their next project. Both these factors diminished a producer's chances of financing a new film. Kluge was even told that he would have to return his subsidy after making *Occasional Work of a Female Slave* (*Gelegenheitsarbeit einer Sklavin*, 1973) because discrepancies were noticed between his original proposal and the finished film. It has been suggested that this was an attempt to censure the film's critical stance on the existing anti-abortion laws (Rentschler 1981–82: 23).

Furthermore, in West Germany representatives of the various political parties sat on the boards of all the television corporations and were therefore in a position to exercise censorship powers. Politicians from the right-wing CDU/CSU in particular have not been reticient in voicing their disapproval of various productions. In 1980, for instance, they blacklisted *The Candidate* (*Der Kandidat*, 1980), a film about the CSU politician Franz-Josef Strauss made by a group of directors which included Kluge and Schlöndorff. The following year Helga Reidemeister reported that she had received rejections from nine television companies when she was trying to raise funding for a feature-length film about Karola Bloch, a Jewish political activist who joined the German Communist Party in the 1930s and lived in East Germany after the war. According to Reidemeister, 'the problem is Karola's past as a CP member, something I can't and don't want to conceal' (in Silberman 1982: 48). She eventually received one quarter of her projected budget and could make only a much condensed version of her original project.

The critically acclaimed *Arbeiterfilme* discussed earlier suffered a similar fate. Although they directly addressed socio-political issues, at times drawing on real-life experiences, they were nevertheless produced as *Autorenfilme*. As a consequence, they blurred the traditional and all-important division in television between factual information and personal opinion and were deemed too radical by the political and television establishments. Political pressure, combined with attacks made in the right-wing press, culminated in the senior personnel at WDR responsible for commissioning the films being replaced and no further *Arbeiterfilme* were commissioned after 1976.

Such censorship reached an unprecedented peak in the mid- to late 1970s in the face of urban terrorism. As terrorist activity had escalated during the 1970s, it resulted in increasing intolerance of dissident viewpoints. In 1972 the *Radikalenerlaß* was passed, a decree colloquially known as the *Berufsverbot* (professional disbarment), which barred political extremists from taking up posts in the civil service. In West Germany this included not only senior staff of government departments, but also teachers, judges, post-office workers, engine drivers, dustmen and gravediggers, who together comprised 16 per cent of the labour force. And gradually other measures were introduced to prohibit, for instance, advocating criminal deeds in a manner hostile to the constitution, or approving of criminal deeds in public. Leftist bookshops, printers and news services were also subjected to repeated investigations, with arrests and confiscation of material not uncommon. Consequently, by 1977 many people felt West Germany had become a police state in which it was impossible to express oppositional viewpoints. In the footage of the terrorists' funeral in *Germany in Autumn* (1978), for instance, we see a banner being carried through the cemetery which states: 'He who attacks West Germany commits suicide.' And according to a contemporary observer: 'Any part of the media that does not cooperate is intimidated by the force of the law. The effect is a public arena, a public opinion, in which no positions deviant from that of the state can exist' (Mayer 1978: 160).

As a result film funding agencies became even more conservative, avoiding any projects that could be construed as politically radical, controversial or socially critical – a situation that Schlöndorff and Böll dramatise in their contribution to *Germany in Autumn*. By 1977 the situation was such that film-makers were beginning to voice their protest, and some threatened to leave the country to work abroad. With typical excess, Fassbinder, for instance, declared: 'If things get any worse, I'd rather be a streetsweeper in Mexico than a film-maker in Germany' (in Elsaesser 1989: 313). Although he did not emigrate, the options for film-makers in the Federal Republic did seem unpromising. If they attempted to address politically sensitive issues they effectively risked 'professional suicide'. Of over 20 scripts addressing the issue of violence in West Germany that had been submitted to the BMI for consideration in 1977, only a handful received any funding (Rentschler 1984: 135). As a member of the reconstituted German Communist Party associated with the overtly political *Arbeiterfilm* genre, Erika Runge simply gave up seeking work with Bavarian television in the 1970s since her film projects were unlikely to be favourably received in this traditionally right-wing area of Germany.

The alternative for film-makers was to seek other sources of funding. The two films which did directly tackle the thorny issue of terrorism at the time, for instance – the collectively-made *Germany in Autumn* (1978) and a later film by Fassbinder, *The Third Generation* (*Die dritte Generation*, 1979) – were both made through private investment. Fassbinder's film did in fact have promises of financial support from WDR television and the West Berlin Senate which were withdrawn during the first week of shooting when the nature of the project became clear. Reflecting on this experience, Fassbinder declared: 'I don't find it such a good idea to try to build up an industry through committees and lobbies – in the end you have to make too many compromises. You just have to do it the capitalist way, on speculation and risk' (in Johnston 1981–82: 68).

The effects of this politically repressive situation on state-subsidised film-making were primarily two-fold. Firstly, it exacerbated a traditional tendency for German film-makers to draw on literary sources. This had already been compounded by funding agencies demanding that film proposals be accompanied by finished scripts. However, in 1976–77 political conservatism resulted in what was perceived to be a *Literatur-verfilmungskrise* – a literature adaptation crisis. In those years there was not only an overwhelming number of literature-based films, but most were adaptations of nineteenth-century classics which appeared to have little contemporary relevance or critical life. A classic example is Helma Sanders-Brahms' film *Heinrich* (1976–77), based on the letters, documents and literature of the nineteenth-century writer Heinrich von Kleist. An elegantly crafted film, it won the top Federal Film Prize for best feature in 1977, but many critics and fellow film-makers vehemently disagreed with the jury's selection of the film for the award.

On the other hand, censorship gave rise to what has been described as a passion for 'oblique approaches and microcosmic case histories' (Dawson 1979: 243). This is particularly evident in films such as von Trotta's *The Second Awakening of Christa Klages* (1977) and *The German Sisters* (1981). Although neither film overtly examine terrorist politics, both films nevertheless allude to the terrorist activity through their protagonists. In the case of *The German Sisters*, it is possible to argue that the film subtly explores the contemporary social problems and their connections to Germany's past through the relationship between two sisters.

A narrative-based film, *The German Sisters* focuses on the relationship between two sisters, Marianne and Juliane, who are loosely based on Gudrun Ensslin and her sister Christiane. In the opening scenes we learn that Marianne has left her husband Werner and son Jan to join a terrorist group, while Juliane lives with her boyfriend Wolfgang, is active in the women's movement and works for a feminist magazine. When Werner commits suicide Juliane is forced to take temporary responsibility for her sister's child. Subsequently the two sisters meet at a museum where Juliane defends her work for a feminist magazine to Marianne as a valid way to effect political change. Juliane finds foster parents for Jan and Marianne goes abroad to work with Arab revolutionaries. On her return Marianne visits Juliane and Wolfgang at their flat in the dead of night, but is rude, inconsiderate and arrogant. When Marianne is arrested, Juliane visits her in prison on several occasions and sends her supplies. Fed up with the way Marianne is dominating their lives, Wolfgang persuades Juliane to go on holiday with him. While they are away, however, they learn of Marianne's death in prison. Back in Germany, Juliane buries her sister and suffers an emotional collapse. Unhappy with the official explanation of suicide, Juliane subsequently embarks on an obsessive investigation of her sister's death and ends her ten-year relationship with Wolfgang. When she finally has the evidence she needs, she phones a newspaper editor only to find they are no longer interested in what is considered yesterday's news. She also takes over caring for Jan after he has been badly burned in a fire thought to have been started by people who discovered his real identity. The film ends with him demanding Juliane tell him about his mother.

To a large extent we only learn about Marianne and her terrorist activities through the eyes of her sister – Juliane, not Marianne, is the central protagonist in the film. And Juliane is represented as experiencing Marianne's politics as an unwelcome intrusion in her life. When she is forced to look after Jan, for instance, she makes it clear to Marianne at their

FIGURE 9 Julianne visits Marianne in prison in *The German Sisters* (1981)

meeting in the museum that she resents being pushed into the mothering role that her sister no longer wants. Marianne's selfish behaviour turns her into the fanatical terrorist of the popular imagination, and during a prison visit Juliane declares Marianne would have been an ardent Hitler supporter if she had been born a generation earlier.

However, rather than show the details of Marianne's capture, the film focuses on how the prison treatment of Marianne becomes increasingly inhumane. Each time Juliane visits her sister, for instance, the physical barrier between them increases – initially they are allowed to embrace and sit at a table, but on Marianne's transfer to a new high security prison a glass panel separates them and they can only speak through a faulty intercom. This, combined with shared memories of their youth which are intercut in flashback sequences, precipitates a growing sympathy in Juliane, which gradually develops into a desire to understand and identify with Marianne.

Although the flashbacks function to humanise Marianne, revealing her to have been a well-behaved 'daddy's girl' – indeed, it was Juliane who was the rebel in their teenage years – they all predate 1968 and hence do not show when and how Marianne became a terrorist. But they do show that she and Juliane, despite their different courses of political action, share the same family and German history. There are flashbacks of them as small children sitting at the family breakfast table, as well as of the teenage sisters in 1955 watching a film about the Nazi concentration camps. Although the act of remembering does not explain the origins of terrorism in Germany, it does suggest a connection between past and present and implies the former shapes and influences the latter. And the final sequence of the film, where Julianne takes Jan home to live with her, suggests that real understanding of the present can only be effected if they come to terms with the past. This is reinforced by the film's German title, which translated literally means 'leaden times', a title von Trotta chose to describe the experience of growing up in West Germany during the 1950s under the burden of an unacknowledged past.

Some critics have suggested, however, that the approaches of such films are so oblique that they have little contemporary relevance. According to Charlotte Delorme, 'if *The German Sisters* were really what it purports to be, it would not have received any support, distribution or exhibition' (1982: 55). Indeed, von Trotta has said in interview that the Ensslin sisters are only 'the point of departure' and that the film in fact contains many of her own memories. Furthermore, as Ellen Seiter has observed:

If [*The German Sisters*] is read as a historical film about Gudrun Ensslin ... why does the film concentrate on the psychological ordeal of the character based on Christiane Ensslin? ... The narrative structure conspicuously excludes information such as Ensslin's involvement in the student movement in Berlin the 1960s ... [and] the terrorists' isolation from the political left in Germany ... We see the consequences of the terrorist actions of Marianne portrayed as personal tragedy – her husband's suicide, her suffering and death in prison, the attack on her son – but we never understand the decisions which led to those actions. (Seiter 1986: 114–15)

But since the director made the film after she had met Christiane Ensslin and the film is actually dedicated to her in the opening title sequence, it is difficult not to interpret the film as dealing in some way with the life of her dead sister Gudrun. This is all the more so, given the clear parallels between the lives of the fictional Marianne and the real-life Gudrun – both are terrorists, both have a sister, both are captured and both are transferred to high-security prisons, where they are eventually found dead. And as if to underscore the parallel, von Trotta includes a shot of the dead Marianne in her coffin virtually identical to the shot of the dead Gudrun that is included in *Germany in Autumn*. Although Seiter is accurate in her observations, these parallels would be unmistakable to a German audience.

Clearly, the film can be read in (at least) two different ways, and which reading viewers make will depend on their knowledge of the socio-political context in which the film was made – hence the change in the film's title for the UK market, and similarly it was changed to *Marianne and Juliane* for the US market – and their expectations of how historical subject matter should be addressed and represented. But censorship at the subsidy level obviously did constrain film-makers and, at one level, the film can be viewed as a measure of the political climate at the time – the film overtly references the terrorist activity but can only do so in a highly personalised form, one which eschews any political analysis of the situation.

Thus, developments during the 1970s appeared to threaten both the New German Cinema's existence and to a certain extent its project of engaging with contemporary reality. The effect of those developments on the film subsidy system had certainly functioned to limit the scope of the new cinema. However, the immediate political crisis had passed by the end of the decade – terrorist activity was on the wane – and the *Literatur-verfilmungskrise* appeared to have likewise passed with only 15 out of 81 films produced in 1979 based on literary sources (Rentscher 1980: 18). When 60 film-makers drew up the Hamburg Declaration at the Hamburg Film Festival in 1979, it seemed to represent a celebration of difficulties overcome since the publication of the Oberhausen Manifesto in 1962. Yet it was not until the mid-1980s that a film was made that directly addressed terrorist politics and the imprisonment, trial and deaths of the captured terrorists: Reinhard Hauff's *Stammheim* (1986), which dramatised the trial of Baader, Meinhof, Ensslin and Raspe from transcripts of the court proceedings. Whereas the high-security prison in von Trotta's film remained nameless, despite the obvious parallel with Stammheim, Hauff could flaunt the name as the title of his film and it won the top prize at the 1986 Berlin Film Festival. But of course, as Juliane finds at the end of *The German Sisters*, the issue had by then ceased to be of contemporary relevance.

The end of an era

Despite the optimism embodied in the Hamburg Declaration, by the mid-1980s innumerable critics had pronounced the demise of the New German Cinema. Whatever had constituted the essence of Germany's new cinema appeared to have evaporated. As one critic expressed it: 'It isn't entirely dead; and yet it is no longer alive' (Kilb 1988: 47). Whilst the increasing constraints of the film subsidy system had played a role – indeed some, such as Edgar Reitz (see Naughton 1992: 9), have argued the new cinema was subsidised to death – it was undoubtedly also partly due to the fact that by then many of the New German Cinema directors were no longer part of or so closely associated with a specifically national cinema. Fassbinder, for instance, who was by far the most prolific and one of the more successful of the cinema's directors, had died in 1982. Andreas Kilb has asserted that 'Whenever one of his films came out, he was already shooting the next one and raising funds for a third' (1988: 49). Hence according to Hans Günther Pflaum, 'Fassbinder kept things moving. … [His] work stimulated other directors. Fassbinder was a great, dynamic element for German cinema' (in Naughton 1992: 10), and he has argued that with his death, more than a director was lost. At the same time Herzog, Schlöndorff, von Trotta, Wenders, Straub and Huillet had all either spent periods working in other countries or emigrated and were turning their attention to non-German subject matter. Wenders, for instance – perhaps the best-known New German Cinema director after Fassbinder – had made *Hammett* (1980–82) and *Paris, Texas* (1983–84) in America and, although they were considered too 'European' for the American market, they were nevertheless made with mostly American actors and in the case of *Hammett* drew on specifically American subject matter. Wenders returned to Berlin to make *Wings of Desire* (*Der Himmel über Berlin*, 1987), but has continued to pursue interests outside Germany with films such as *Tokyo Ga* (1985), *Until the End of the World* (*Bis ans Ende der Welt*, 1991), *Buena Vista Social Club* (1999) and *The Million Dollar Hotel* (1999). Similarly, Schlöndorff had made *Swann in Love* (*Un amour de Swann/Eine Liebe von Swann*, 1983) in France and *Death of a Salesman* (1985) in the US, while von Trotta had also broadened her scope with *Three Sisters* (*Paura e amore*, 1988) set in Italy and *The Return* (*L'Africana*, 1990) in France. Indeed, it was not until the early 1990s with her film *The Promise* (*Das Versprechen*, 1994) about a German-German love affair, prompted by the fall of the Berlin Wall, that von Trotta returned to German-specific subject matter.

But a combination of other factors – both national and international – was also involved and helped to undermine much of what had made the New German Cinema films distinctive and identifiable as a quality national cinema. Whilst it is not possible to discuss all those factors here, a key one was in fact the role of television in the new cinema. In the wake of the Film and Television Agreement of 1974 television began to assume a crucial role within West German cinema and by the 1980s very few films were produced without television funding of some kind. On the one had, as Elsaesser asserts, television can be regarded as 'the patron saint of the new independent feature' (1976: 14). It had not only given the new directors vital support when alternative forms of financing were highly limited and helped develop a quality national cinema, some of its commissioning policies had also given rise to highly innovative film work. *Das kleine Fernsehspiel* department at ZDF, for instance, extended a high degree of creative freedom to film-makers and were prepared to 'sponsor total amateurs' (Johnston and Ellis 1982: 62). Jutta Brückner described her experiences as follows:

> It's an excellent department ... They really let you do things the way that you want to ... And they've got a wonderful arrangement known as 'Kamerafilm'; you get a very small sum of money, but it's put entirely at your disposal. The only thing you ever have to do is deliver a film on the date agreed. (in Harbord 1981–82: 48)

On the other hand, however, as television assumed this crucial role, other funding agencies tended to follow its lead – if a project had been rejected by one or more television corporations, other funding committees were often reluctant to award grants. A further effect of the Film and Television Agreement was that closer and more regular working relationships were developed between film-makers and television commissioning editors and pushed the film-makers increasingly into the role of programme-makers, often encouraged to tailor their work for broadcast on the small screen as much as for theatrical release. Although the new directors considered themselves to be *film* directors rather than *television* directors and regarded the cinema as the natural home for their work, the Film and Television Agreement was consequently criticised for resulting in 'uncinematic' films. Indeed, as television became the major funder and exhibitor of such work, from a critical viewpoint it raises the question of whether the films could be considered as constituting a 'cinema'. In fact, the television stations were on the whole supportive of the *Autorenfilm* – in many ways the concept fitted in with their policies of commissioning freelancers and their remit as public corporations to mediate a plurality of opinions – but in reality the concept of the *Autor*, so central to the identity of the New German Cinema, diminished in importance. According to Elsaesser, this was compounded by the fact that television's increasing role in West German cinema coincided with a period when freelance television workers were organising themselves in order to secure permanent posts within the institutions in preference to being celebrated as artists.

But political developments also played a crucial role. Through the 1970s the Social Democrats had remained in power with the support of the Free Democratic Party (FDP). In 1982, however, the FDP switched their support to the right-wing CDU/CSU and in doing so forced an election which returned the CDU/CSU to power. This had far-reaching consequences for the film sector since the ultra-conservative Friedrich Zimmermann became Minister of the Interior and he attempted to assume absolute control over how film funds were administered. Under his guidance film policy was revised to clearly favour commercial, big-budget, Hollywood-style 'entertainment' projects over any form of artistic experimentation or concern for cultural 'quality'.

As he declared: 'The taxpayer does not wish to be provoked, he wants to be entertained' (quoted in Moeller 1984–85: 66). As if in confirmation of his assertion, one of the most successful German films in the 1980s was *Otto – The Film* (*Otto – der Film*, 1985), a light-hearted slapstick comedy co-directed by Otto Waalkes and Fassbinder's former cameraman Xaver Schwarzenberger, in which Waalkes, the popular television comedian, plays a bumbling, hapless East Friesian freshly arrived in the big city. The film attracted an audience of over eight million and won a prize for record attendance figures. And indeed, by the late 1980s trade magazines were reporting increases in attendances at West German cinemas.

With such an emphasis on 'entertainment', the more experimental and innovative film-makers were the obvious and most immediate casualties of the revised film policy. During Zimmermann's first year in office, for instance, he withdrew aid already awarded to Herbert Achternbusch's *The Ghost* (*Das Gespenst*, 1982) and refused a subsidy for the film-maker's later project *The Wandering Cancer* (*Der Wanderkrebs*, 1984) because they were supposedly 'an affront to the moral consensus and offended religious values' (Naughton 1991: 10). Elfi Mikesch and Monika Treut also had BMI funding withdrawn from their film project *Seduction: The Cruel Woman* (*Verführung: die grausame Frau*, 1984–85) shortly after it had been awarded on the basis that the film was considered pornographic. However, as the 1980s progressed and with subsequent revisions to the Film Development Act (FFG) in 1987, there was a further shift in film policy towards supporting 'two or three big productions a year and not much else' (Naughton 1992: 8), with a greater stress on raising production values, maximising audiences and increasing profitability. Indeed, a new stipulation was introduced during the 1980s, that 'whoever has been funded three times and does not manage at least once to see at least twenty percent of a film's production cost returned at the box-office will not be permitted further funding contracts' (quoted in Naughton 1991: 11). Although not even half of the films supported by the Film Development Board had achieved that level of return, the requirement was subsequently raised to 30 per cent.

These political developments also coincided with a shift back to more commercial and industrial modes of film-making. As some of the new directors had achieved international success, it opened up possibilities for American distributors co-producing German films. And that success on the international scene also meant that West German cinema increasingly became part of the international film and television industries, with a concomitant loss of some its national specificity. At the same time, as the sheer number of films being produced rose – especially to meet the demands of television programmers – industrial modes of production almost of necessity began to reemerge. This was compounded by changes in film funding policy during the 1980s which discouraged directors from taking on multiple roles in the way they had done during the early years of the New German Cinema. For a while the concept of the *Autorenfilm* remained a necessary fiction, holding everything together, but it had become clear that the artisanal mode of production which had characterised much of the new cinema could not indefinitely sustain a quality national cinema. If West German cinema was to keep pace with the international film and television industries, it periodically required major investment and the experience of working on larger budget productions. As Schlöndorff had pointed out as early as 1972:

> It simply makes good sense for a film industry to undertake three or four times a year projects which cost DM5 to 8 million, because this way a large number of technicians and other professionals are employed and trained, it is a healthy shot in the arm for the industry itself ... [It] not only raises the industry's infrastructure to the latest stage of technology, but can also be used to break into the World Market. (in Elsaesser: 17)

Thus, even by the early 1980s, the German film industry had started to move into bigger budget productions utilising the latest technology. Films like Wolfgang Petersen's *The Boat* (*Das Boot*, 1981) and his later *The Neverending Story* (*Die Unendliche Geschichte*, 1984), for instance, drew on latest special effects technology to bring German film-making up to an international commercial standard and make it more able to compete in the international export market.

And, of course, the cost of producing films rose so dramatically during the 1980s that national funding initiatives alone were frequently inadequate. As a result film-makers often had to turn to other countries to find co-funding or to apply to the new pan-European agencies to help meet the shortfall. In order to meet the criteria of such funders, however, film projects are often required to demonstrate a broader European or international appeal and can lose their cultural specificity.

Both *Three Sisters* (1988) and *The Return* (1990) by von Trotta are, for instance, Italian, French and West German co-productions. The former is set in Italy and is about three sisters – 'a Chekhov's *Three Sisters* for nowadays' according to the director. The eldest, Valia, is a literature academic who embarks on an affair with Massimo, a married science professor. Massimo, however, soon throws Valia over for her sister Maria, who is married to Frederico, a television comedian. The youngest sister, Sandra, is still a student, studying to become a doctor of medicine. Although the film sets up a tension between art and science, suggesting the former possesses eternal values of some kind which science in the form of nuclear technology and television threatens but cannot totally destroy, this sub-plot remains undeveloped. Rather, the film concentrates with depressing seriousness on the emotional agonies to which the various characters subject each other, the deceptions they practice, and their inability to find real happiness.

The Return, set in Paris, also focuses on the relationship between three people – this time, two women and a man. Anna is in hospital with an unspecified but life-threatening illness. She persuades her husband, Michel, to write to her friend Marthe who is working in Africa and ask her to return to Paris. Marthe arrives and as the film unfolds we discover that she and Anna used to be lovers. After they split up Marthe met Michel, who in turn fell in love with and married Anna. Anna now believes that her illness is a form of punishment for hurting Marthe by taking Michel away from her. As this film also examines the way its characters hurt each other, swap partners and are unable to satisfactorily resolve their situation, it is almost as if von Trotta has simply refilmed *Three Sisters*, changing the names.

Although some international co-productions can be successful – *Jean de Florette* (1986) and *Manon des Sources* (1986), both directed by Claude Berri, are good examples – both of von Trotta's films can be regarded as prime examples of projects which, by trying to transcend cultural and national boundaries, have become totally characterless. Suzi Feay's description of *Three Sisters* in her review of the film for London's listings magazine *Time Out* adequately describes them both: 'It's a Euro production: multi-lingual cast puréed in a blender and poured out like glop' (in Knight 1992: 158). The almost complete lack of critical response to or debate around *Three Sisters* and *The Return* provides a sharp contrast to the critical interest aroused and debate generated by her earlier film discussed above, *The German Sisters*.

Conclusion

Although it is beyond the scope of this introductory study to cover the changing conditions of film production, distribution and exhibition at both a national and international level more fully, the above discussion demonstrates that by the 1980s a number of factors had combined to dramatically transform the cultural, economic and political landscape in which the New German Cinema directors were working. And of course, the changes discussed above were exacerbated from the late 1980s onwards by the emergence of media conglomerates, the growth of cable and satellite broadcasting and the development of digital technologies. Thus, just as a set of historically specific circumstances and conditions had brought the New German Cinema into being, it is possible to argue that another set of equally historically specific circumstances meant that much of what made the cinema distinctive – and had attracted so much critical attention and acclaim – had disappeared and hence brought about its demise.

That said, younger German film-makers have continued to emerge, such as Monika Treut and Doris Dörrie, both of whom began to attract critical attention during the 1980s, and more recently Tom Tykwer who attracted considerable international attention with his first feature *Deadly Maria (Die tödliche Maria*, 1993) and subsequently with *Run Lola Run (Lola rennt*, 1998). And the cultural imperative to promote a new German cinema has remained at some levels. The annual International Forum of Young

Film, for instance, which is held in conjunction with the Berlin Film Festival continues to include a 'New German Film' section.

Dörrie, in particular, has been something of a success story and suggests that some of the imperatives informing and shaping the New German Cinema have survived. Born between 10 and 20 years after those directors most closely associated with the New German Cinema, she made a string of documentaries and feature films for various television stations after leaving film school. Such were the audience ratings for one of these, *In Between* (*Dazwischen*, 1981), that a German television company decided to back her first cinema feature, *Straight Through the Heart* (*Mitten ins Herz*, 1983). But more significantly, in the mid-1980s she enjoyed unexpected critical *and* box-office success with her comedy about middle-class male mores, *Men* (*Männer*, 1985).

Men was seen by six million viewers within the first six months of its release – outgrossing *Rambo* at the German box-office according to the film's promotional material. Moreover, Dörrie was prepared for the strident German left-wing press to tear the film apart. But if anything male critics identified with her characters – the 1968 generation turned yuppies – and one was moved to assert after seeing the film that 'the German film appear[s] to have a future again',[1] while another critic attributed her with winning 'unaccustomed popularity for the German film'.[2] The film enjoyed a similar success in the US and brought her a number of offers from Hollywood.

And if anything her success has continued and, as is so often the case in today's multi-media world, straddles a number of fields, including authoring several novels, short story collections and children's books, and directing opera performances. However, she is not alone in this, as Werner Herzog, for instance, has also turned his hand to opera direction. But of perhaps greater significance is her involvement in film education. She teaches at Munich's Television and Film School (HFF), where she has been in charge of the screenwriting programme. Once again, she is not an isolated example: Reinhard Hauff has been the head of Berlin's Film and Television Academy (DFFB) for a number of years and other New German Cinema directors, together with younger directors – including Dörrie and Treut – have held teaching posts in American universities. This means critically acclaimed German directors are in key positions to encourage, influence and promote the upcoming generation of new film-makers both at home and abroad. While the perception may be that the 'essence' of the so-called New German Cinema had disappeared by the mid-1980s, some longer term benefits have nevertheless emerged for the country's film culture and its reputation abroad.

At the same time, it is possible to argue that the international critical acclaim garnered by the New German Cinema films has also generated greater interest in German cinema generally. While early accounts of the new cinema tend to represent the films by Fassbinder, Herzog, Wenders and others as bursting upon an otherwise barren German film scene, subsequent accounts have located the films within wider historical, cultural and political traditions. One of the first to do this was Eric Rentschler's edited anthology, *German Film and Literature: Adaptations and Transformations*, first published in 1986. Although Rentschler stressed that the volume was 'anything but definitive' (p. 5), it draws on film texts from every decade from the 1910s through to the 1980s to demonstrate that there has been an interaction between film and literature throughout the history of German cinema – it was not something peculiar to the New German Cinema era. Taking another approach, in 1993 Sandra Frieden *et al* published a two-volume anthology of essays 'looking at the broad spectrum of German Cinema through the category of gender' (back cover). Entitled *Gender and German Cinema*, the publication deals with many New German Cinema films, but also includes a section specifically called 'Film History Before New German Cinema' which looks back at the silent era as well as at Nazi cinema.

Other books have explored more contemporary connections. Richard McCormick's illuminating study, *Politics of the Self* (1991), for instance, discusses six literary and film texts in the context of feminism, postmodernism, the West German student movement and the country's cultural and political upheaval since the 1960s, while Ingeborg Majer O'Sickey and Ingeborg von Zadow's *Triangulated Visions* (1998) includes essays about women working in East German cinema. Still other books have started to address areas of German film history that have traditionally received relatively little sustained and in depth study. For instance, Heide

Fehrenbach has examined German cinema of the 1950s in her *Cinema in Democratizing Germany: Reconstructing National Identity after Hitler* (1995) to explore the 'complex political uses of film ... during a period of abrupt transition to democracy' (back cover). And Eric Rentschler turned his attention to the popular entertainment films of the Third Reich in *The Ministry of Illusion: Nazi Cinema and its Afterlife* (1996).

While interest in the New German Cinema obviously persists – as evidenced by John Davidson's *Deterritorializing the New German Cinema* (1999) – the result of this growing body of literature has been to locate and contextualise it within the entirety of German cinema history. Hence in 1999 Thomas Elsaesser (together with Michael Wedel) was able to produce a very useful reference book, *The BFI Companion to German Cinema*, which covers the complete span of German-speaking cinema from the 1890s through to the 1990s, while three years later Sabine Hake published her *German National Cinema* similarly covering the entire twentieth century. And given that both Elsaesser's and Hake's volumes take us firmly into the post-New German Cinema era – with Hake's book including a chapter specifically addressing post-unification cinema – what becomes important is not so much the perceived demise of New German Cinema, but what that new cinema has contributed to the future of German film.

NOTES

Introduction

1   Sandford's book was originally published in 1980 in hardback. The edition cited is the paperback one, published the following year.

Chapter One

1   For the general flavour of reviews, see Brown 1980; N. Wapshott (1980) 'The boy who decided to stop growing', *The Scotsman*, 17 May; A. Sarris (1980) 'Banging the Tin Drum Slowly', *The Voice*, 21 April; T. Milne (1980) 'Beating the Tin Drum', *The Observer*, 18 May; and J. Simons (1980) 'Boom, Boom, Oskar makes a real hit!', *Daily Express*, 17 May.

Chapter Two

1   According to Brustellin *et al.* (1988: 133): 'Frau Wilde is a character who appears in Kluge's collection of stories, *Neue Geschichten. Hefte 1-18. "Unheimlichkeit der Zeit."*' (Frankfurt am Main: Suhrkamp, 1978), pp. 313–15.

2   See T. O'Sullivan *et al.* (eds) (1994) *Key Concepts in Communication*. Second edition. London: Routledge, 192, where myth is defined as

'A widely and variously used term referring to a culture's way of understanding, expressing and communicating to itself concepts that are important to its self-identity as a culture'.

3 Habermas' article originally appeared in *Die Zeit* in July 1986 under the title 'Eine Art Schadensabwicklung'. An English translation of it was published in *New German Critique* (1988) 44, Spring/Summer, pp. 25–39, under the title 'A Kind of Settlement of Damages (Apologetic Tendencies)'.

Chapter Three

1 Robin Detje, 'Deutschland ist blau', *Die Zeit*, 3–10 January 1992, p. 46.

2 Katrin Müller, 'Quartett am Bett', *Tip*, 21 January–3 February 1988.

BIBLIOGRAPHY

The bibliography lists works cited in the text and is also designed to point to useful further reading. The annotated list of 'essential reading' highlights works considered to be of particular importance to the study of New German Cinema although many valuable contributions are also to be found under 'secondary reading'.

ESSENTIAL READING

Corrigan, T. (1994) *New German Film: The Displaced Image*. Revised and Expanded Edition. Bloomington and Indianapolis: Indiana University Press.
Using close analyses of nine films, Corrigan provides a detailed exploration of the relationship between New German Cinema and Hollywood.
Elsaesser, T. (1989) *New German Cinema: A History*. Basingstoke and London: MacMillan.
This is the single most comprehensive study of the New German Cinema.
____ (ed.) with M. Wedel (1999) *The BFI Companion to German Cinema*. London: BFI Publishing.
A useful reference book which locates New German Cinema and its directors within the entirety of German cinema history.
Hartnoll, G. and V. Porter (eds) (1982) *Alternative Filmmaking in Television:*

ZDF – A Helping Hand, Dossier 14. London: BFI Publishing.
  Gives a detailed account of one aspect of the interaction between West German film and television.
Johnston, S. (1979–80) 'The Author as Public Institution. The "New" Cinema in the Federal Republic of Germany', *Screen Education*, 32–3, 67–78.
  Provides a history and analysis of the role of the concept of 'Autor' in New German Cinema.
Kaes, A. (1989) *From 'Hitler' to 'Heimat': The Return of History as Film.* Cambridge, Mass. and London: Harvard University Press.
  Through extensive analyses of five films, Kaes examines the shifting relationship to Germany's Nazi past that occurred during the 1970s.
Knight, J. (1992) *Women and the New German Cinema.* London and New York: Verso.
  Provides an in-depth discussion of the contribution made by women film-makers to the New German Cinema.
McCormick, R. W. (1991) *Politics of the Self: Feminism and the Postmodern in West German Literature and Film.* Princeton: Princeton University Press.
  A complex and illuminating study which contextualises German cultural activity within the political upheaval in West Germany since the 1960s.
O'Sickey, I.M. and I. von Zadow (eds) (1998) *Triangulated visions: Women in Recent German Cinema.* Albany: State University of New York Press.
  Collection of essays offering analyses of films by critically neglected film-makers, including women working in the former East Germany.
Rentschler, E. (1984) *West German Film in the Course of Time.* Bedford Hills, New York: Redgrave Publishing Company.
  Examines the US reception of the New German Cinema and other contexts from which the new cinema emerged.

SECONDARY READING

Andersen, B. (1991) *Imagined Communities: Reflections on the Origin and Spread of Nationalism.* Revised edition. London and New York: Verso.
Bergfelder, T., E. Carter and D. Göktürk (eds) (2002) *The German Cinema Book.* London: BFI Publishing.

Bergmann, C. (1984) 'Sheer Madness: An Interview with Margarethe von Trotta', *Cineaste*, 13, 4, 47.

Bhabha, H.K., ed. (1990) *Nation and Narration*. London and New York: Routledge.

Bordwell, D. (1985) 'Art-Cinema Narration', in Bordwell, *Narration in the Fiction Film*. London and New York: Routledge, 205–33.

Bratton, J., J. Cook and C. Gledhill (eds) (1994) *Melodrama: Stage Picture Screen*. London: BFI Publishing.

Brown, G. (1980) 'A life of many meanings', *Financial Times*, 14 May.

Brustellin, A., R. W. Fassbinder, A. Kluge, V. Schlöndorff, B. Sinkel (1988) 'Germany in Autumn: What is the Film's Bias? (1978)', in E. Rentschler (ed.) *West German Filmmakers on Film: Visions and Voices*. New York and London: Holmes and Meier, 132–3.

Burckner, C. (1987) 'Critical Observations on the Changed Situation of the German Film d'Auteur and the Possibilities it has of Reaching the Viewer', in Goethe Institute (ed.) *Basis Film: A Berlin Model of Film Production and Distribution*. London: Goethe Institute, II/1–6.

Caughie, J. (1992) 'Becoming European – Art Cinema, Irony and Identity', in D. Petrie (ed.) *Screening Europe*. London: BFI Publishing, 32–44.

Chalmers, M. (1985) 'Heimat: Approaches to a Word and a Film', *Framework*, 26–7, 90–101.

Clarke, G. (1978) 'Seeking Planets that do not Exist: The New German Cinema is the Liveliest in Europe', *Time*, 20 March.

Collins, R. and V. Porter (1981) *WDR and the Arbeiterfilm: Fassbinder, Ziewer and others*. London: BFI Publishing.

Corrigan, T. (1983) *New German Film: The Displaced Image*. Austin: University of Texas Press.

Davidson, J. (1999) *Deterritorializing the New German Cinema*. Minneapolis and London: University of Minnesota Press.

Dawson, J. (1979) 'The Sacred Terror', *Sight and Sound*, 48, 4, 242–5.

_____ (1981) 'A Labyrinth of Subsidies', *Sight and Sound*, 50, 1, 14–20.

Delorme, C. (1982) 'Zum Film "Die bleierne Zeit" von Margarethe von Trotta', *Frauen und Film*, 31, February, 52–5.

Discourse (1983), 6, Fall.

Eidsvik, C. (1979) 'Behind the Crest of the Wave: An Overview of the New

German Cinema', *Literature/Film Quarterly*, 7, 3, 167–81.

Elsaesser, T. (1976) 'The Post-war German Cinema', in T. Rayns (ed.) *Fassbinder*. London: BFI Publishing, 1–16.

_____ (1988) 'The Heimat-Film' in Goethe Institute (ed.) *Deutscher Heimatfilm*. London: Goethe Institute, II/1–14.

_____ (1994) 'Putting on a Show: The European Art Movie', *Sight and Sound*, 4, 4, 23–7.

_____ (1996) *Fassbinder's Germany: History Identity Subject*. Amsterdam: Amsterdam University Press.

Everett, W. (ed.) (1996) *European Identity in Cinema*. Exeter: Intellect Books.

Fassbinder, R. W. (1975) 'Fassbinder on Sirk', trans. T. Elsaesser, *Film Comment*, 11, 6, November/December, 22–4.

Fehrenbach, H. (1995) *Cinema in Democratizing Germany: Reconstructing National Identity after Hitler*. Chapel Hill and London: The University of North Carolina Press.

Franklin, J. (1983) *New German Cinema: From Oberhausen to Hamburg*. London: Columbus Books.

Frieden, S., R. W. McCormick, V. R. Petersen and L. M. Vogelsang (eds) (1993) *Gender and German Cinema: Feminist Interventions, Volumes 1 and 2*. Providence and Oxford: Berg.

Gerber, H. (ed.) (1977) *Kuratorium junger deutscher Film 1965–1976. Zielsetzung, Entwicklung, Förderungsweise*. Munich: Kuratorium Junger Deutscher Film, e.V.

Ginsberg, T. and K. Thompson (1996) *Perspectives on German Cinema*. New York: G.K. Hall & Co.

Graf, A. (2002) *The Cinema of Wim Wenders*. London and New York: Wallflower Press.

Guback, T. H. (1969) *The International Film Industry*. Bloomington: University of Indiana Press.

Habermas, J. (1988) 'A Kind of Settlement of Damages (Apologetic Tendencies)', *New German Critique*, 44, Spring/Summer, 25–39.

Hake, S. (2002) *German National Cinema*. London and New York: Routledge.

Harbord, P. (1981–82) 'Interview with Jutta Brückner', *Screen Education*,

40, Autumn/Winter, 48–57.

Herbst, H. (1985) 'New German Cinema, 1962–83: A View From Hamburg', *Persistence of Vision*, 2, Fall, 69–75.

Hurd, G. (ed.) (1984) *National Fictions: World War Two in British Films and Television*. London: BFI Publishing.

Johnston, S. (1981–82) 'A Star is Born: Fassbinder and the New German Cinema', *New German Critique*, 24–5, Fall/Winter, 57–72.

____ and J. Ellis (1982) 'The Radical Film Funding of ZDF', *Screen*, 23, 1, 60–73.

Kilb, A. (1988) 'Rainer Doesn't Live Here Anymore', *Film Comment*, 24, 4, July-August, 47–9.

Kuzniar, A.A. (2000) *The Queer German Cinema*. Stanford, CA: Stanford University Press.

Literature/Film Quarterly (1979) 7, 3.

Literature/Film Quarterly (1985) 13, 4.

Mayer, M. (1978) 'The German October of 1977', *New German Critique*, 13, Winter, 155–63.

Moeller, H. B. (1984–85) 'West German Women's Cinema: The Case of Margarethe von Trotta', *Film Criticism*, 9, 2, Winter, 51–66.

Naughton, L. (1991) 'A Very German Film Industry', *Film News*, March, 10–11.

____ (1992) 'Fassbinder: ten years on...', *Film News*, August, 10–11.

Neale, S. (1981) 'Art Cinema as Institution', *Screen*, 22, 1, Spring, 11–39.

New German Critique (1981–82) 24–5, Fall/Winter.

Persistence of Vision (1985), 2, Fall.

Petrie, D. (ed.) (1992) *Screening Europe: Image and Identity in Contemporary European Cinema*. London: BFI Publishing.

Pflaum, H. G. (1990) *Germany on Film: Theme and Content in the Cinema of the Federal Republic of Germany*. Detroit: Wayne State University Press.

Pflaum, H. G. and H. H. Prinzler (1979) *Film in der Bundesrepublik Deutschland. Der neue deutsche Film, Herkunft/Gegenwärtige Situation: Ein Handbuch*. Munich: Fischer Taschenbuch Verlag.

____ (1983) *Cinema in the Federal Republic of Germany. The New German Film, Origins and Present Situation: A Handbook*. Bonn: Inter Nationes.

Phillips, K. (ed.) (1984) *New German Filmmakers*. New York: Frederick

Ungar.

Quarterly Review of Film Studies (1980) 5, 2, Spring.

Rentschler, E. (1980) 'Deutschland im Vorherbst: Literature Adaptation in West German Film', *Kino (German Film)*, 3, Summer, 11–19.

_____ (1981–82) 'American Friends and the New German Cinema: A Study in Reception', *New German Critique*, 24–5, Fall/Winter, 7–35.

_____ (ed.) (1986) *German Film and Literature: Adaptations and Transformations*. New York and London: Methuen.

_____ (ed.) (1988) *West German Filmmakers on Film: Visions and Voices*. New York and London: Holmes and Meier.

_____ (1996) *The Ministry of Illusion: Nazi Cinema and its Afterlife*. Cambridge, Mass. and London: Harvard University Press.

Sandford, J. (1981) *The New German Cinema*. London: Eyre Methuen.

Sanders-Brahms, H. (1980) *Deutschland, bleiche Mutter: Film-Erzählung*. Hamburg: Rowohlt.

Seiter, E. (1986) 'The Political is Personal: Margarethe von Trotta's "Marianne and Juliane"', in C. Brundson (ed.) *Films for Women*. London: BFI Publishing, 109–16.

Silberman, M. (ed.) (1982) 'Film and Feminism in Germany Today', *Jump Cut*, 27, July, 41–53.

_____ (ed.) (1984) 'German Film Women', *Jump Cut*, 29, 49–64.

_____ (ed.) (1985) 'German Women's Film Culture', *Jump Cut*, 30, 63–9.

_____ (1995) *German Cinema: Texts in Context*. Detroit, MI: Wayne State University Press.

Sorlin, P. (1991) *European Cinemas, European Societies*. London and New York: Routledge.

Thomsen, C. B. (1997) *Fassbinder: The Life and Work of a Provocative Genius*. London and Boston: Faber and Faber.

Torpey, J. (1988) 'Introduction: Habermas and the Historians', *New German Critique*, 44, Spring/Summer, 5–24.

Wenders, W. (1988) 'That's Entertainment: Hitler (1977)', in E. Rentschler (ed.) *West German Filmmakers on Film: Visions and Voices*. New York and London: Holmes and Meier, 126–31.

_____ (1989) *Emotion Pictures*. London: Faber and Faber.

Wide Angle (1980) 3, 4.

INDEX

SHORT CUTS

THE SHORT CUTS series is a comprehensive library of introductory texts covering the full spectrum of Film Studies including genres, critical concepts, film histories/movements and film technologies.

With concise discussion of contemporary issues within historical and cultural context and the extensive use of illustrative case studies, this list of study guides is perfectly suited to building an individually-styled library for all students and enthusiasts of cinema and popular culture.

The series will grow to over forty titles; listed here are the first waves of this ambitious attempt to systematically treat all the major areas of undergraduate Film Studies.

> "TAILOR-MADE FOR A MODULAR APPROACH TO FILM STUDIES ...
> AN INDISPENSABLE TOOL FOR BOTH LECTURERS AND STUDENTS."
>
> PROFESSOR PAUL WILLEMEN, UNIVERSITY OF ULSTER

THE HORROR GENRE
FROM BEELZEBUB TO BLAIR WITCH

Paul Wells

The Horror Genre is a comprehensive intro-duction to the history and key themes of the genre. The main issues and debates raised by horror, and the approaches and theories that have been applied to horror texts are all featured. In addressing the evolution of the horror film in social and historical context, Paul Wells explores how it has reflected and commented upon particular historical periods, and asks how it may respond to the new millennium by citing recent innovations in the genre's development, such as the urban-myth narrative underpinning *Candyman* and *The Blair Witch Project*.

144 pages   1-903364-00-0   £12.99 pbk

> 'A valuable contribution to the body of teaching texts available ... a book for all undergraduates starting on the subject.'
>
> Linda Ruth Williams, University of Southampton

THE STAR SYSTEM
HOLLYWOOD'S PRODUCTION OF POPULAR IDENTITIES

Paul McDonald

The Star System looks at the development and changing organisation of the star system in the American film industry. Tracing the popularity of star performers from the early 'cinema of attractions' to the internet universe, Paul McDonald explores the ways in which Hollywood has made and sold its stars. Through focusing on particular historical periods, the key conditions influencing the star system in silent cinema, the studio era and the New Hollywood are discussed and illustrated by case studies of Mary Pickford, Bette Davis, James Cagney, Julia Roberts, Tom Cruise, and Will Smith.

144 pages   1-903364-02-7   £12.99 pbk

"A very good introduction to the topic filling an existing gap in the needs of teachers and students of the subject."

Roberta Pearson, University of Wales, Cardiff

SCIENCE FICTION CINEMA
FROM OUTERSPACE TO CYBERSPACE

Geoff King and Tanya Krzywinska

From lurid comic-book blockbusters to dark dystopian visions, science fiction is seen as both a powerful cultural barometer of our times and the product of particular industrial and commercial frameworks. The authors outline the major themes of the genre and explore issues such as the meaning of special effects and the influence of science fiction cinema on the entertainment media of the digital age. The book concludes with an extensive case-study of *Star Wars Episode I: The Phantom Menace*.

144 pages   1-903364-03-5 £12.99 pbk

"The best overview of English-language science-fiction cinema published to date ... thorough, clearly written and full of excellent examples. Highly recommended."

Steve Neale, Sheffield Hallam University

EARLY SOVIET CINEMA
INNOVATION, IDEOLOGY AND PROPAGANDA

David Gillespie

Early Soviet Cinema examines the aesthetics of Soviet cinema during its golden age of the 1920s, against a background of cultural ferment and the construction of a new socialist society. Separate chapters are devoted to the work of Sergei Eisenstein, Lev Kuleshov, Vsevolod Pudovkin, Dziga Vertov and Alexander Dovzhenko. The author places primary focus on the text, with analysis concentrating on the artistic qualities, rather than the political implications, of each film.

144 pages   1-903364-04-3   £12.99 pbk

"An excellent book … lively and informative. It fills a significant gap and deserves to be on reading lists wherever courses on Soviet cinema are run."

Graham Roberts, University of Surrey

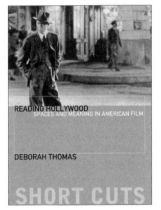

READING HOLLYWOOD
SPACES AND MEANINGS IN AMERICAN FILM

Deborah Thomas

Reading Hollywood examines the treatment of space and narrative in a selection of classic films including *My Darling Clementine*, *Its a Wonderful Life* and *Vertigo*. The author employs a variety of arguments in exploring the reading of space and its meaning in Hollywood cinema. Topics covered include the importance of space in defining genre (such as the necessity of an urban landscape for a gangster film to be a gangster film); the ambiguity of offscreen space and spectatorship (how an audience reads an unseen but inferred setting) and the use of spatially disruptive cinematic techniques such as flashback to construct meaning.

144 pages   1-903364-01-9   £12.99 pbk

"Amongst the finest introductions to Hollywood in particular and film studies in general … subtler, more complex, yet more readable than most of its rivals, many of which it will displace."

Professor Robin Wood

DISASTER MOVIES
THE CINEMA OF CATASTROPHE

Stephen Keane

Disaster Movies provides a comprehensive introduction to the history and development of the disaster genre. From 1950s sci-fi B-movies to high concept 1990s millennial movies, Stephen Keane looks at the ways in which the representation of disaster and its aftermath are borne out of both contextual considerations and the increasing commercial demands of contemporary Hollywood. Through detailed analyses of such films as *Airport, The Poseidon Adventure, Independence Day* and *Titanic*, the book explores the continual reworking of this, to-date, undervalued genre.

144 pages   1-903364-05-1   £12.99 pbk

"Providing detailed consideration of key movies within their social and cultural context, this concise introduction serves its purpose well and should prove a useful teaching tool."

Nick Roddick

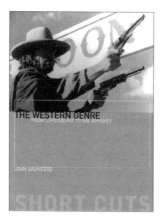

THE WESTERN GENRE
FROM LORDSBURG TO BIG WHISKEY

John Saunders

The Western Genre offers close readings of the definitive American film movement as represented by such leading exponents as John Ford, Howard Hawks and Sam Peckinpah. In his consideration of such iconic motifs as the Outlaw Hero and the Lone Rider, the author traces the development of perennial aspects of the genre, its continuity and its change. Representations of morality and masculinity are also foregrounded in consideration of the genre's major stars John Wayne and Clint Eastwood, and the book includes a number of detailed analyses of such landmark films as *Shane, Rio Bravo, The Wild Bunch* and *Unforgiven*.

144 pages   1-903364-12-4   £12.99 pbk

"A clear exposition of the major thematic currents of the genre providing attentive and illuminating reading of major examples."

Ed Buscombe. Editor of the BFI Companion to the Western

PSYCHOANALYSIS AND CINEMA
THE PLAY OF SHADOWS

Vicky Lebeau

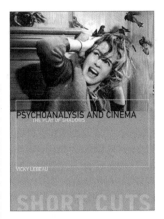

Psychoanalysis and Cinema examines the long and uneven history of developments in modern art, science and technology that brought pychoanalysis and the cinema together towards the end of the nineteenth century. Vicky Lebeau explores the subsequent encounters between the two: the seductions of psychoanalysis and cinema as converging, though distinct, ways of talking about dream and desire, image and illusion, shock and sexuality. Beginning with Freud's encounter with the spectacle of hysteria on display in fin-de-siècle Paris, this study offers a detailed reading of the texts and concepts which generated the field of psychoanalytic film theory.

144 pages   1-903364-19-1   £12.99 pbk

"A very lucid and subtle exploration of the reception of Freud's theories and their relation to psychoanalysis's contemporary developments – cinema and modernism. One of the best introductions to psychoanalytic film theory available."

Elizabeth Cowie, University of Kent

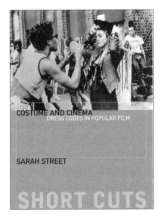

COSTUME AND CINEMA
DRESS CODES IN POPULAR FILM

Sarah Street

Costume and Cinema presents an overview of the literature on film costume, together with a series of detailed case studies which highlight how costume is a key signifier in film texts. Sarah Street demonstrates how costume relates in fundamental ways to the study of film narrative and mise-en-scène, in some cases constituting a language of its own. In particular the book foregrounds the related issues of adaptation and embodiment in a variety of different genres and films including *The Talented Mr Ripley*, *Desperately Seeking Susan*, *Titanic* and *The Matrix*.

128 pages   1-903364-18-3   £12.99 pbk

"A valuable addition to the growing literature on film and costume ... engagingly written, offering a lucid introduction to the field."

Stella Bruzzi, Royal Holloway College, University of London

MISE-EN-SCÈNE
FILM STYLE AND INTERPRETATION

John Gibbs

Mise-en-scène explores and elucidates constructions of this fundamental concept in thinking about film. In uncovering the history of mise-en-scène within film criticism, and through the detailed exploration of scenes from films such as *Imitation of Life* and *Lone Star*, the author makes the case for the importance of a sensitive understanding of film style, and provides an introduction to the skills of close reading. This book thus celebrates film-making and film criticism alive to the creative possibilities of visual style.

128 pages   1-903364-06-X   £12.99 pbk

"An immensely readable and sophisticated account of a topic of central importance to the serious study of films."

Deborah Thomas, University of Sunderland

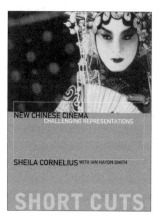

NEW CHINESE CINEMA
CHALLENGING REPRESENTATIONS

Sheila Cornelius with Ian Haydn Smith

New Chinese Cinema examines the 'search for roots' films that emerged from China in the aftermath of the Cultural Revolution. Sheila Cornelius contextualises the films of the so-called Fifth Generation directors who came to prominence in the 1980s and 1990s such as Chen Kaige, Zhang Yimou and Tian Zhuangzhuan. Including close analysis of such pivotal films as *Farewell My Concubine*, *Raise the Red Lantern* and *The Blue Kite*, the book also examines the rise of contemporary Sixth Generation underground directors whose themes embrace the disaffection of urban youth.

144 pages   1-903364-13-2   £12.99 pbk

"Very thorough in its coverage of the historical and cultural background to New Chinese Cinema ... clearly written and appropriately targeted at an undergraduate audience."

Leon Hunt, Brunel University

SCENARIO
THE CRAFT OF SCREENWRITING

Tudor Gates

Scenario presents a system of logical analysis of the basic structures of successful screenplays, from initial plot-lines to realised scripts. All the essential building blocks are discussed in depth: the need for a strong premise; the roles of protagonist and antagonist; the orchestration of plot, characters and dialogue leading to a clear resolution. Written by a highly-experienced and successful screenwriter, this is a book which not only instructs first-time writers how to go about their work but also serves as a valuable check-list for established authors, and for actors, directors and teachers, in their task of deconstructing and assessing the value of the material placed before them.

144 pages   1-903364-26-4   £12.99 pbk

"This is an immensely readable introduction to the craft of screenwriting and is very helpful for budding screenwriters."

Alby James, Northern Film School

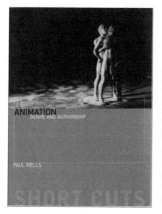

ANIMATION
GENRE AND AUTHORSHIP

Paul Wells

Animation: Genre and Authorship is an introductory study which seeks to explore the distinctive language of animation, its production processes, and the particular questions about who makes it, under what conditions and with what purpose. Arguably, animation provides the greatest opportunity for distinctive models of 'auteurism' and revises generic categories. This is the first study to look specifically at these issues, and to challenge the prominence of live action movie-making as the first form of contemporary cinema and visual culture.

144 pages   1-903364-20-8   £12.99 pbk

"Absolutely excellent. Clearly introduces areas which do not have an adequate literature."

David Huxley, Manchester Metropolitan University

WOMEN'S CINEMA
THE CONTESTED SCREEN

Alison Butler

Women's Cinema provides an introduction to critical debates around women's film-making and relates those debates to a variety of cinematic practices. Taking her cue from the ground-breaking theories of Claire Johnston and the critical tradition she inspired, Alison Butler argues that women's cinema is a minor cinema which exists inside other cinemas, inflecting and contesting the codes and systems of the major cinematic traditions from within. Using canonical directors and less established names as examples, ranging from Chantal Akerman to Moufida Tlatli, the book argues that women's cinema is unified in spite of its diversity by the ways in which it reworks cinematic conventions.

144 pages   1-903364-27-2   £12.99 pbk

"An excellent introduction ... engages with complex ideas in a beautifully written and tightly focused manner."

Carrie Tarr, University of Kingston-upon-Thames

BRITISH SOCIAL REALISM
FROM DOCUMENTARY TO BRIT GRIT

Samantha Lay

British Social Realism details and explores the rich tradition of social realism in British cinema from its beginnings in the documentary movement of the 1930s to its more stylistically eclectic and generically-hybrid contemporary forms. Samantha Lay examines the movements, moments and cycles of British social realist texts through a detailed consideration of practice, politics, form, style and content, using case studies of key texts including *Listen To Britain*, *Saturday Night and Sunday Morning*, *Letter To Brezhnev*, and *Nil By Mouth*. The book considers the challenges for social realist film practice and production in Britain, now and in the future.

144 pages   1-903364-41-8   £12.99 pbk

"Without doubt the best introduction to this distinctive and fascinating genre that any film student could hope to read"

Film Ireland

FILM EDITING
THE ART OF THE EXPRESSIVE

Valerie Orpen

Film Editing offers an analysis of editing in the sound film that considers the craft as an expressive strategy rather than a mere technique. It reveals that editing can be approached and studied in a similar way to other aspects of film such as mise-en-scène. Studies on editing or montage tend to focus on silent cinema, yet this book claims that such examinations should also consider the role of the soundtrack. The aim is to examine the way in which editing can produce meaning in a wider context, as a crucial element of the overarching design and vision of a film. Includes detailed studies of Scorsese's *Raging Bull*, Hitchcock's *Rear Window* and Godard's *A Bout de Souffle*.

144 pages   1-903364-53-1   £12.99 pbk

"An exceptionally intelligent book about a notoriously elusive subject: editing in various kinds of narrative film-making"
Professor Brian Henderson, University at Buffalo, SUNY

THE AVANT-GARDE FILM
FORMS, THEMES AND PASSIONS

Michael O'Pray

The Avant-Garde Film examines the variety of concerns and practices that have comprised the long history of avant-garde film. It covers the developments of experimental film-making since the modernist explosion in the 1920s in Europe through to the Soviet film experiments, the American Underground cinema and the French New Wave, structuralism and contemporary gallery work of the young British artists. Through in-depth case-studies, the book also examines varied analytical approaches to the films themselves – from abstraction (Richter, Ruttmann) through underground subversion (Jack Smith, Warhol) to experimental narrative (Deren and Antonioni).

144 pages   1-903364-56-6   £12.99 pbk

"An excellent job of providing a very readable introduction ... A good starting point for anyone interested in avant-garde film"
Julia Knight, University of Luton

PRODUCTION DESIGN
ARCHITECTS OF THE SCREEN

Jane Barnwell

Production Design explores the role of the production designer through a historical overview
that maps out landmark film and television de-
signs. From the familiar environs of soap operas
to the hyper-realism of *Trainspotting* and the dis-
orientation of *Velvet Goldmine*, design is integral
to understanding moving-image text. The book
investigates questions of authenticity in detail,
props, colours and materials. The design codes
of period drama are examined and contrasted
with more playful productions of the past, and
key examples range from musicals of the 1930s
to cult films of the 1990s. The book also includes
interviews with leading production designers.

144 pages   1-903364-55-8 £12.99 pbk

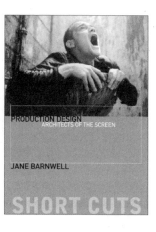

"For anybody curious about the history of production design and for designers
interested in the preoccupations of predecessors and peers, this book is
more comprehensive than anything before – masses of research and opinion
analysed with real insight and understanding."

Stuart Craig, Production Designer

EARLY CINEMA
FROM FACTORY GATE TO DREAM FACTORY

Simon Popple & Joe Kember

Early Cinema explores the period 1895 to 1914
when cinema emerged as the leading form of visual culture and established itself as a worldwide
institution. This book introduces the student
to the study of cinema as a series of aesthetic,
technological, cultural, ideological and economic
debates while exploring new and challenging
approaches to the subject. The authors make
use of the latest research in this field presenting
both critical and practical advice for the student
through a series of case studies.

144 pages   1–903364–58–2 £12.99 pbk

"Bringing new perspectives and rigour to the study of film and popular
culture, there is a real need for the up-to-date introduction that Popple and
Kember provide."

Prof. Ian Christie, Birkbeck College, London